Soviet Sources
of Military Doctrine
and Strategy

Soviet Sources *of* Military Doctrine *and* Strategy

William F. Scott

PUBLISHED BY

Crane, Russak &
Company, Inc.

NEW YORK

National Strategy
Information Center, Inc.

Soviet Sources of Military Doctrine
and Strategy
Published in the United States by
Crane, Russak & Company, Inc.
347 Madison Avenue
New York, N.Y. 10017

Copyright © 1975 by
National Strategy Information Center, Inc.
111 East 58th Street
New York, N.Y. 10022

Library Edition: ISBN 0-8448-0709-5

Paperbound Edition: ISBN 0-8448-0710-9

LC 75-18537

Strategy Paper No. 26

Printed in the United States of America

Table of Contents

Preface

Even so efficient a totalitarian system as the Soviet Union must usually communicate with its people through open channels. In addition to obvious exploitation of the mass media for purposes of propaganda and indoctrination, the public press is employed for the instruction of Party cadres, government officials, and military personnel to an extent not usually appreciated in the West. To be sure, secret channels of communication abound; but they are difficult to use when large numbers of people are involved. In most cases, the only alternative is to rely on more or less freely available newspapers, journals, and books for the dissemination of important information of all kinds.

This is also the case with respect to the broad outlines of Soviet military doctrine and strategy, which we might otherwise assume to be too sensitive a subject—in a society given to preternatural secrecy —to treat so openly. But millions of officers and other personnel need to know the substance of such matters, if they are to function effectively, and the only feasible means of reaching them in most instances is through the open press. Nor is there any serious doubt as to the essential reliability of these publications. It would be inconceivable that the Moscow regime would risk deluding its own military personnel on such a mass scale, simply in order to confound the West. In any case, much of the material is independently verifiable—for example, by observation of the weapon systems developed by the Soviet military, which necessarily bear a close relation to proclaimed doctrine and strategy.

The purpose of the remarkable monograph that follows is to provide an annotated bibliography of Soviet newspapers, journals, and some 168 books containing significant material on military doctrine and strategy between the years 1960 and 1974, a period during which Soviet military thinking was revolutionized, not least by the introduction of nuclear weapons into the arsenals of the Soviet Armed Forces. Much of these materials are, of course, available only in Russian, and therefore directly accessible only to those familiar with the language. But in the course of his annotation, the author also provides sufficient commentary on the substance to give some indication of the extent to which Soviet military doctrine and strategy have evolved over the past 15 years. The result is a unique tool for all those seriously interested in studying the subject in depth.

The author, Colonel William F. Scott (USAF, Ret.) was graduated from West Point in 1943. He holds a Master's degree from Georgetown University, and a Ph.D. in Political Science from George Washington University. During his distinguished military career, Colonel Scott served two tours as senior United States Air Attache in Moscow. He is the author of numerous articles on Soviet military doctrine, strategy, and tactics.

Frank R. Barnett, *President*
National Strategy Information Center, Inc.

July 1975

1

Introduction

The famed Moscow Summit Meeting in May 1972, which ended with the signing of a limited SALT agreement, prepared the groundwork for a series of further negotiations. SALT, MBFR, and European Security meetings may last for years. A major question resulting from the negotiations would be whether or not they will bring about changes in Soviet military doctrine and strategy. And if changes in doctrine and strategy do occur, what will be their impact upon the development, production, and deployments of Soviet weapon systems?

Before any possible shift in Soviet military thought can be determined by the Western observer, it is first necessary that there be some common agreement on what were the basic tenets of Soviet doctrine and strategy at the time of, and prior to, the Moscow Summit. From 1960 to 1975, scholars in the United States held differing views with respect to both the content and the meaning of Soviet military writings. Hence, the corpus of such writings published over the past 15 years needs to be reexamined. The purpose of this monograph is to provide an annotated bibliography of the Soviet newspapers, journals, and books that contain significant writings on military doctrine and strategy over the period 1960-74.

Are the development, production, and deployment of Soviet weapon systems reflected in such military writings? The test is very simple to make. A lead time of six to ten years is required between the date a study on a new weapon system is initiated and the date on which it is finally deployed into operational units. Weapon systems in the hands of Soviet troops in 1974 were the result of decisions made by the Kremlin between 1962 and 1968. From various publications, such as the annual *Military Balance*, published by the British Institute of Strategic Studies, we have a good idea of the Soviet order of battle, including types and numbers of weapon systems deployed. We can check Soviet writings on military subjects during the 1962-68 period, and determine whether or not the doctrine and strategy advocated correspond to the types of weapon systems that actually were in existence and manned by 1974. Any analyst, reading Soviet military writings which may be available in American universities and research centers, can easily make this judgment for himself.

This monograph will attempt to identify the most important Soviet newspapers, journals, and books likely to be of interest to students of Soviet military affairs, and published between 1960 and 1974, especially those dealing with or reflecting Soviet concepts of military doctrine and strategy. The most significant books in these categories are those which have been issued in the "Officer's Library" series;[1] recommended for further reading in the 1971 *Officer's Handbook*;[2] listed as basic reference in the latest edition of the *Bolshaya Encyclopedia*;[3] included in the "Soldier's Bookshelf," as given in the Ministry of Defense's annual publication, *Calendar of a Soldier*;[4] and those nominated for a Frunze Prize.[5]

A few books on Party-military subjects, issued by the Academy of Sciences Publishing House and other publishers, are also listed, as well as a number of writings containing various resolutions and instructions of the Communist Party, and a basic text on Marxism-Leninism. The purpose here is to present the decrees of the Party Congresses affecting the military, and the fundamentals of Marxist-Leninist philosophy. A number of miscellaneous writings on various

---

[1] The "Officer's Library" series of books was announced in December 1964 by Voyenizdat, the publishing house of the Ministry of Defense. Some 17 books were issued in this series. The purpose is "to arm the reader with a knowledge of the fundamental changes which have taken place in recent years in military affairs."
[2] The *Officer's Handbook* is one of the "Officer's Library" series of books. At the end of each chapter is a recommended reading list for further study.
[3] The *Bolshaya Sovietskaya Encyclopedia* is regarded as the most authoritative Soviet reference work available. The first volume of the new edition appeared in 1970; and by 1974, the first 16 volumes had been issued.
[4] The *Calendar of a Soldier* has been issued by Voyenizdat since the mid-1960s. One section is entitled "The Soldier's Bookshelf," and contains the major works published by Voyenizdat.
[5] In March 1965, the Council of Ministers of the USSR approved the award of a "Frunze Prize" each year for "excellent military or military historical works."

military matters will also be given in the bibliography. These are intended to show how doctrine and strategy are reflected in other publications of the military press.

The key books to note, however, are those of the "Officer's Library" series, nominations for the Frunze Prize, recommendations in the *Officer's Handbook,* inclusions in the "Soldier's Bookshelf," and basic references in the *Bolshaya Encyclopedia.*

The Nature of Soviet Military Writings

Soviet military publications available to Western scholars contain relatively little about their own new technology, weapon systems, and order of battle. They do provide Party-military views on military doctrine and strategy. The reason for this is that the Soviet leadership regards the indoctrination of the Soviet Armed Forces as a matter of major importance. Since 1962, military writings have emphasized the need for all members of the Soviet Armed Forces to understand fully the "revolution in military affairs." In general, openly published materials are intended for the political-military indoctrination of Soviet military personnel.

One experienced observer of Soviet military affairs notes that the views appearing in the classified Soviet journal, *Military Thought,* and in other "nonpublicly available Soviet sources correspond with and endorse those published in the open military press."[6] The unclassified writings are primarily intended for the education and training of all Soviet military personnel, from generals to new recruits. Specific publications are written for various ranks and different intellectual levels.

The Western analyst, accustomed to freedom of the press, may wonder where are the Soviet writers who do not agree with the points of view expressed in the books, journals, and newspapers listed. Such freedom of the press does not exist in the Soviet Union. A few Soviet intellectuals may circulate their "samizdat" manuscripts

---

[6] Garthoff, Raymond L., *Soviet Strategy in the Nuclear Age,* revised edition, Praeger Paperbacks, New York, 1926, p. 271.

among a very small group of readers. Eventually, some may find their way to the outside world, where they are published. To date, no military theoretical writing in this "samizdat" category has been identified to Western scholars.

In the United States and in most other nations, it is possible for any individual, without any official governmental sanction, to write and publish articles and books on military matters. Such individuals may support or oppose the existing military order. Dissent is not uncommon. Even newspaper columnists may become self-appointed authorities on military subjects, and be widely read and quoted. This is not the case in the Soviet Union. All military writings are carefully reviewed and controlled, and nothing is published without censorship. At times, there may be discussions or views that propose modifications to existing concepts. Such writings are carefully identified. There may be some differences expressed in military science, which may even be encouraged by the Party-military leadership. As analysts of Soviet military thought will note, however, there cannot be any argument in the Soviet press about military doctrine. The reason for this will be readily apparent when the reader understands what Soviet spokesmen mean when they speak of doctrine, strategy, military science, and military art.

2

Political-Military Spokesmen

With the possible exception of the Minister of Defense, the military rank of an author is no indication of the relative importance of the writing. An article or a book by a colonel, who also might be a Professor and a Doctor of Philosophical Sciences, may be as important as a work by a marshal, general, or admiral. Frequently, new ideas or new concepts will first be introduced at the colonel or lieutenant colonel level.

Senior Soviet Officers

The most authoritative Soviet military spokesman is the Minister of Defense, followed by the Chief of the General Staff. These two officers would be expected to write on general matters of military doctrine and strategy. Marshal Malinovskiy's pamphlet, *Vigilantly Stand Guard Over the Peace*, published in 1962, was considered a basic document on doctrine and strategy even after the ouster of Khrushchev in 1964 and Malinovskiy's death in 1967. This tract was without rival until Marshal Grechko's equally famed work, *On Guard Over the Peace and the Building of Communism*, was issued in 1971. This, in turn, has now been superseded by the Minister of Defense's book, *The Armed Forces of the Soviet State,* published in 1974.

The Chief of the General Staff may also write on doctrine and strategy affecting all of the Soviet Armed Forces. But this would not normally be the case for the other Deputy Ministers of Defense. For example, a First Deputy Minister of Defense and Commander-in-Chief of the Warsaw Pact Forces would be expected to write on matters affecting the Warsaw Pact. In like manner, other Deputy Ministers and Commanders-in-Chief generally would write on their particular service or organization. In their writings or speeches, they will reflect the main points of doctrine and strategy, although they may stress the role of one particular service, or the value of one particular weapon system.

Within the General Staff, the Military Science Administration plays perhaps the key role in developing doctrinal and strategic concepts. The Academy of the General Staff also has an important role in the development of doctrine. Spokesmen associated with either of these organizations are particularly important.

Faculty of the Frunze Military Academy

The staff of this academy is concerned with "combined arms" training. Publications written by the Frunze Academy faculty deal with tactics instead of doctrine. Many of the faculty members have advanced degrees in military science. It is important that the analyst be familiar with their writings in order to see how doctrine and strategy, applicable to all services of the Soviet Armed Forces, are reflected in Ground Forces publications.

Faculty of the Lenin Military-Political Academy

The faculty of the Lenin Military-Political Academy plays a role that has no counterpart within the United States or other non-Communist nations. For this reason, the writings of these officers frequently may be misunderstood. The Academy is under the cognizance of the Main Political Administration of the Soviet Army and Navy, an organization that operates with the rights of a department of the Central Committee of the Communist Party. Thus, the spokesmen of the Academy must combine Party ideology with military and foreign policy considerations. To equip them for this task, those faculty members whose works are frequently published have advanced degrees in the philosophical sciences, which in the Soviet Union essentially means Marxism-Leninism. They take the decisions reached by the Party and the military and place them in a Marxist-Leninist framework. Two of the better-known writers in this group are Colonels Rybkin and Bondarenko, one a Doctor of Philosophical Sciences and the other a "Candidate"—an advanced degree that roughly corresponds to the Ph.D. in the United States.

Institutes Under the Academy of Sciences

In the Soviet Union, military strategy comes under the purview of the social sciences. The 23rd Communist Party Congress, held in March-April 1966, decreed that work in the social sciences must be improved. During the Congress, an article entitled "On Contemporary Military Strategy," by Marshal Sokolovskiy, appeared in *Communist of the Armed Forces*. In this article, Sokolovskiy made reference to research institutes in Western nations, such as the RAND Corporation, the Hudson Institute, and the Institute for Strategic Studies in England. He suggested that the work of these institutes was very important to the development of Western military thought. A year later, in 1967, the Institute of the USA was established in Moscow.

Two of the most articulate of Soviet military writers left the General Staff to join this new institute. One, Colonel V. V. Larionov, had been the composing editor of all three editions of *Military Strategy*. His academic credentials are impressive—a Candidate degree in Military Science and a Doctorate in History. Another is the distinguished General Colonel N. A. Lomov, for many years a General Staff officer and a professor at the General Staff Academy, now Head of the Military Science Society of the Central Officers Club.

As the Institute of the USA was getting underway, an older and very prestigious organization, the Institute of World Economy and International Relations (IMEMO) was taking an equal interest in military matters. A former General Staff officer and Doctor of History, Colonel V. M. Kulish, joined the international relations staff

of this institute. Another military writer with an established reputa-
tion, Colonel V. V. Glazov, also became a member of the organization.

Doctors Kulish and Larionov, as well as Colonel Glazov, had
attended a very important conference on military doctrine held in
May 1963 to discuss "The Essence and Content of Soviet Military
Doctrine," at which both Kulish and Larionov delivered major
speeches. Interestingly, Larionov at the time stressed the difficulty
in defining military doctrine, military science, and military strategy.
Kulish restated the definition that "military doctrine represents the
view officially adopted in the state on the character, form, and methods of waging a future war, and also on the structuring of the Armed
Forces and preparation of the country for war."[7]

Members of these institutes probably do not write on Soviet military
doctrine and strategy as such. Rather, their primary function is to
study the capitalist world "for determining the most effective ways
and means to insure socialism's victory over capitalism."[8] They frequently investigate very topical items such as SALT and MBFR.
Many of their writings are well worth reading, especially if the reader
is aware of their former positions in the Soviet Armed Forces.

[7] "Conference on Soviet Military Doctrine," *Military Historical Journal*, No. 10, October
1963, pp. 121-126. By 1974, Colonel Larionov had returned to the General Staff, and Colonel
Kulish had left IMEMO.
[8] Zagladin, V., "The Revolutionary Process and the International Policy of the CPSU,"
Kommunist, No. 13, September 1972, p. 15.

3

Basic Sources

Newspapers

The main advantage of newspapers as a source is that they are the most timely. Next to radio and television, newspapers are the first to note important speeches of Party and military spokesmen. Such speeches might indicate a shift in policy, or show the guidelines that are to be followed in the future. On the other hand, newspapers are not likely to provide the insights that can be gained from an analysis of journals and books.

In so far as daily newspapers are concerned, *Red Star* (Krasnaya Zvezda) is by far the most important to the student of Soviet military affairs. It is the official newspaper of the Ministry of Defense. It is published every day except Monday, and is found throughout the Soviet Union. It may contain articles on doctrine, strategy, or tactics written by the Minister of Defense, senior military leaders, faculty members of the Lenin Military-Political Academy, or by staff members of the Institute of the USA or of IMEMO. A second military newspaper is *Soviet Patriot* (Sovetskiy Patriot), an official organ of DOSAAF (Volunteer Organization for Cooperation with the Army, Aviation, and the Fleet.) Other military newspapers do exist, such as those published by each of the military districts, but they are not readily available.

Pravda and *Izvestia* occasionally print articles on matters of military doctrine and strategy. Generally, such articles are written by senior military commanders to appear on special occasions, such as Armed Forces Day, Tank Day, Navy Day, and so on. Readers should be aware of the occasion on which these articles appear, and recognize that Admiral Gorshkov, Commander-in-Chief of the Soviet Navy, will stress the accomplishments of the Navy on Navy Day, or General Tolubko, Commander-in-Chief of the Strategic Rocket Forces, will seek to glorify the rocket troops on Rocket Troops and Artillery Day.

As *Red Star* represents the Ministry of Defense, *Pravda* is the official newspaper of the Central Committee of the Communist Party of the Soviet Union, and *Izvestia* of the Soviet government. The military analyst should read *Red Star*, and scan *Pravda* and *Izvestia*. Other Soviet newspapers should be checked from time to time, especially on military holidays.

On rare occasions, interesting and fairly significant articles will show up in unexpected places. In 1965, *Nedelya* (The Week), the magazine section of *Izvestia*, published an article by General Colonel Shtemenko entitled, "The Queen of the Battlefield Yields Her Crown." At this time, the general opinion among US analysts was that the Soviet Armed Forces were changing Khrushchev's former emphasis on nuclear weapons. The theme of Shtemenko's article, as given in the title, was completely at variance with what US analysts expected.[9]

Journals as a Source

Communist of the Armed Forces (Kommunist Vooruzhennykh Sil) is by far the most important Soviet journal, openly published, for the non-Communist military analyst. It appears twice monthly, and is the official journal of the Main Political Administration.

---

[9] In 1965, following the ouster of Khrushchev, the opinion of many followers of the Soviet military scene was that the Soviets would lessen their emphasis on nuclear weaponry. Shtemenko's article, as did all other Soviet articles and books at the time, restated the new doctrine that had been announced by Khrushchev in January 1960.

In its "political studies" section, specific directions are given to political instructors in units, directing how many hours will be given to the study of a particular theme, and even dividing the study hours into seminars, reading periods, and lecture periods. The "political studies" themes for each new study year as published since 1962 have been as follows:

1. October 1974, "The CPSU on Raising the Defense Power of the Motherland, Education of the Soviet People in the Spirit of Vigilance and Constant Military Preparedness to Defend the Gains of Socialism." Lavrent'yev, V.

2. October 1973, "The Demands of the CPSU and the Soviet Government in Supporting High Vigilance and Constant Combat Readiness of the Armed Forces of the USSR." Cherednichenko, N., Colonel.

3. September 1972, "Defense of the Fatherland, Service in the Armed Forces—the High and Honored Obligation of Each Soviet Citizen." No author given.

4. September 1971, "Defense of the Fatherland, Service in the Soviet Armed Forces—the High and Honored Obligation of Each Soviet Citizen." Lisenkov, M., Colonel, Candidate of Historical Sciences.

5. October 1970, "Imperialism—the Source of War." Doubnya, N., Colonel, Candidate of Historical Sciences.

6. October 1969, "The Character and Features of Modern War." Kozlov, V., Lieutenant Colonel, Candidate of Philosophical Sciences.

7. September 1968, "Imperialism—the Source of War. The Imperialist Aggressors, Headed by the USA, the Worst Enemy of Peace and Security of the People." Kondratkov, T., Lieutenant Colonel, Candidate of Philosophical Sciences.

8. October 1967, "The Character and Features of Modern War." Kondratkov, T., Lieutenant Colonel, Candidate of Philosophical Sciences.

9. October 1966, "Serve the Motherland as the Great Lenin Devised." No author given.

10. October 1965, "The Leninist Idea of Defending the Socialist Fatherland." No author given.

11. October 1964, "The Features and Character of World Nuclear War." Palevich, I., Colonel, and Poznyak, I.

12. October 1963, Magazine unavailable.

13. October 1962, "The Character and Features of Modern War." Palevich, I., Colonel.

Contributors to *Communist of the Armed Forces* will range from the Minister of Defense and other high Party, government, or military officials to faculty members of the military academies. The student of Soviet military affairs cannot afford to overlook this journal.

The Military History Journal (Voyenno-Istoricheskii Zhurnal) probably is second in importance. It is considered the best written and best edited of all the Soviet military publications. The study of military history plays a very important role in the formulation of Soviet military doctrine and strategy. For example, new writings on World War II constantly are being introduced, not simply for the purpose of informing the reader about that war, but rather to show specifically how certain lessons still are applicable. Thus, military history is used to indoctrinate and to teach lessons on current doctrine, strategy, and tactics.

Four of the five services—the Aerospace Defense Forces (PVO), the Ground Forces, the Air Forces, and the Navy—publish journals that are readily available. (In all probability, the Strategic Rocket Forces also have a journal, although copies have never appeared for public subscription.) These journals are very useful to any student of Soviet military affairs. But they do not often contain articles of significance on doctrine or strategy. At times, they do have articles on tactics, or relate doctrine to a particular service. Their greatest value is to demonstrate how basic doctrine and strategy are reflected in their articles.

The Soviet service journals are as follows:

Aviation and Cosmonautics (Aviatsiya i Kosmonavtika). This is the official journal of the Soviet Air Forces. It is published monthly. Note that it also deals with space, and one or more Soviet Air Forces Cosmonauts are on its editorial board.

Herald of the PVO (Vestnik Protivovozdushnoi Oborony). This monthly journal is for the Aerospace Defense Forces. Since PVO consists of interceptor aircraft, surface-to-air missiles, and radar units, this journal cuts across the traditional service lines of the US Armed Forces.

Military Herald (Voyenniy Vestnik). This is the monthly journal of the Soviet Ground Forces.

Naval Collections (Morskoi Sbornik). This is the monthly journal of the Soviet Navy. In format, it is somewhat similar to its US counterpart, the *Naval Institute Proceedings*.

Other major military journals are as follows:

The Rear and Supply of the Soviet Armed Forces (Tyl i Snab-zheniye Sovietskikh Voorzhennykh Sil.) The Soviet Rear Services are a major command, and cut across service lines. Their journal is published monthly.

Equipment and Armaments (Tekhnika i Vooruzheniye). At the Ministry of Defense level, there is a Deputy Minister for Armaments. Each service also appears to have a Deputy Commander-in-Chief whose business is armaments. Each service has engineering officers, who are designated as such. This journal would appear to be of interest to engineering officers of all services. It is published monthly.

Military Knowledge (Voyennye Znaniye). This is the journal of DOSAAF, an organization with a membership of several million

Soviet youth. The United States does not have anything to compare with this huge paramilitary organization, which is active throughout the Soviet Union. Articles in this journal frequently deal with civil defense and general miiltary themes.

Starshina-Sergeant (Starshina-Serzhant). The monthly illustrated journal of the Ministry of Defense for the noncommissioned officer. It contains technical articles and stories. In 1974, the name of this journal was changed to the *Banner Carrier* (Znamenosets).

Soviet Soldier (Sovietskiy Voin). Like the *Communist of the Armed Forces*, this journal is issued twice monthly by the Main Political Administration of the Soviet Army and Navy. It is written primarily for enlisted personnel. It stresses the patriotic qualities of the Soviet soldier and the glory of the Communist fatherland.

Agitator's Notebook (Bloknot Agitatora). This is issued twice monthly by the Main Political Administration of the Soviet Army and Navy, for use by the "agitator and propagandist." (AGITPROP halls are found throughout the Soviet Union.) The booklet is very valuable as an indication of what the Soviet people are told at Party and Komsomol meetings.

Military Thought (Voyennaya Mysl'). This is a restricted or classified journal. A number of US writers on Soviet military doctrine and strategy have made reference to this publication. Current numbers are not generally available to the Western researcher. Reprints of older articles frequently can be found.

Soviet Military Review. This is a monthly journal, published in English, French, and Arabic—but not printed in Russian. It is intended for foreign consumption. In general, the articles published in this magazine are not found in publications intended for Soviet readership. Occasionally, an abridged reprint from *Red Star* (Krasnaya Zvezda) or a Soviet military journal will appear. Any person reading this journal as a major source of Soviet military thought would likely be misled.

Nonmilitary Journals of Interest to the Military Analyst

The Soviet military analyst should study newspapers that are intended for general reading throughout the Soviet Union. He should also scan a number of journals intended for Soviet civilian readers in order to appreciate the position the military holds within the total Party-governmental structure.

Kommunist, the official journal of the Communist Party, is perhaps the best single journal for this purpose. From time to time, it may have important articles by the Minister of Defense or other key military figures. Sometimes the rank or position of a military writer will not be noted. Apparently this is not with any intent to deceive. Rather, it appears that it is assumed that the reader of *Kommunist* would recognize the name of A. A. Grechko as that of the Minister of Defense.

USA (SSHA) is the monthly journal issued by the Institute of the USA. The purpose of this institute is to study the United States, and the journal is designed to inform the Soviet readership about the United States. There are times when the articles apparently are intended as a dialogue with some group or other in the United States. A number of the articles are on military-political subjects, such as SALT, Mutual and Balanced Force Reductions (MBFR), and European Security. As already noted, some of the most articulate and profound Soviet military strategists are on the staff of this institute.

World Economy and International Relations (Mirovaya Ekonomika i Mezhdunarodnoye Otnosheniye) is the monthly journal of the Institute of World Economy and International Relations (IMEMO). The purpose of this institute is to study the economics and international relations of the capitalist world. It examines all of the non-Communist world, not simply the United States. Like *USA*, this journal frequently has articles on military-political subjects. Also, like the Institute of the USA, IMEMO has on its staff a number of former military strategists.

Although both *USA* and *MEIMO* are printed only in the Russian language, each contains a table of contents in English as well as in

Russian. It appears that both journals are intended for both Soviet and foreign readers.

International Affairs (Mezhdunarodnaya Zhizn) is in a category of its own. It is issued monthly by the Znaniye Publishing House, and is printed in Russian, English, and French. It is found in many cities throughout the Soviet Union which are frequented by foreigners. The Znaniye (Knowledge) Society, which prints *International Affairs*, has 2,319,000 members in the USSR, and numbers 1,300 academicians and corresponding members of the Academy of Science in its ranks. Its purpose is to popularize science. The Society is very active in promoting the exchange of delegations.

Books

Books are the most important single source of Soviet military doctrine and strategy. As already noted, all writings on military subjects reflect some official view, and have a purpose. Their main drawback is that they are not topical. It is seldom that a book can be issued in less than eight months after the manuscript is submitted to the publisher. A delay of 14 to 18 months is not uncommon between the time the manuscript is prepared and the book is available at bookstores. This delay may suggest that the contents have been given very careful consideration.

The Ministry of Defense has its own publishing house, Voyenizdat, and issues the majority of the books written on military subjects. The second most important military publisher is DOSAAF. This Soviet paramilitary group has approximately 9,000,000 regular members, with several million additional Soviet citizens using DOSAAF facilities.

From time to time, significant writings on military doctrine and strategy are issued by other publishing houses, such as that of the Academy of Sciences or the Political Publishing House. Books printed by other than military publishers are of particular interest. They serve to confirm Party-military ties, and indicate what is intended for the nonmilitary reader.

Books issued by the Military Publishing House seldom come out unannounced. For example, *Communist of the Armed Forces* generally has an article each fall on the books that are expected to appear over the following 12 months. At the military bookstores throughout the Soviet Union, brochures often are available, providing information for ordering future books, and giving purpose, price, and number of pages. The average Soviet reader can find out more easily about projected books than can his counterpart in the United States.

In the bibliography that follows, books will be listed by the year in which they were published. The year 1960 appears a logical date on which to start. According to Soviet military spokesmen, this year marked a significant change in Soviet military affairs. As one leading theorist notes:[10]

> Three stages can be distinguished in the development of the Soviet Armed Forces and military art after World War II. The first encompasses the immediate postwar years, 1945-53; the second, from the end of 1953 to 1959; and the third stage began in 1960.

Khrushchev's announcement of the formation of the Strategic Rocket Troops, which took place in January 1960, marked the beginning of the third stage. The Soviet spokesman continues:

> In the third stage of the postwar period, from the beginning of 1960, the qualitative transformations in the Army and in military affairs continued. A new service of the Armed Forces was created and developed, the Strategic Rocket Forces, and the nuclear rocket weapon and other continually improved means of armed struggle were widely introduced in the necessary amounts into all the services of the Armed Forces.

The bibliography begins with Khrushchev's speech of January 14, 1960, delivered before the Fourth Session of the Supreme Soviet

---

[10] Strokov, A. A., Colonel, Doctor of Philosophical Sciences, Professor, *The History of Military Art*, Voyenizdat, 1966, p. 590. For a translation of this portion of the book, see Kintner, W. R., and Scott, H. F., *The Nuclear Revolution in Soviet Military Affairs*, University of Oklahoma Press, Norman, Oklahoma, 1968, pp. 195-234.

of the USSR. Before starting this bibliography, however, two earlier works may be of particular interest to Western readers. Both were sent to the printers in December 1959, less than a month before Khrushchev made his speech. The books are:

Rybkin, Ye. I., Major, Candidate of Philosophical Sciences, *War and Politics* (Voyna i Politika), Voyenizdat, 1959, 144 pages.

This book first brought the name of Ye. I. Rybkin to the attention of Western students. Rybkin's basic thesis is that the nuclear weapon had brought about a revolution in military affairs. He discusses military doctrine, strategy, and military science in a manner that is significantly different from most Soviet writers of the 1950s, except possibly a few authors whose articles were published in *Military Thought*. Throughout the 1960s and into the 1970s, Rybkin's articles appeared to establish guidelines that other writers would follow. His 1965 work, "On the Nature of Nuclear Rocket War," published in *Communist of the Armed Forces*, served as an excellent barometer to forecast the direction that Soviet weaponry was to take over the next decade. At the time, most Western analysts thought that Rybkin was a "Red Hawk," expressing opposition both to the Party and military leadership. The unity and continuity of Soviet military thought is well documented in a 1973 work, *Scientific-Technical Progress and the Revolution in Military Affairs*. Editor of this book is General Colonel N. A. Lomov, a Professor and a consultant to the Institute of the USA. Rybkin, now a Colonel and Doctor of Philosophical Sciences, was one of the contributors. Rybkin's 1959 book can be compared with his views published after the signing of the SALT I agreements.

Grigorenko, P. G., General Major, Candidate of Military Sciences, Editor, *Methods of Military-Scientific Research* (Metodika Voyenno-Nauchnovo Issledovaniya), Voyenizdat, 1959, 268 pages.

In the mid-1960s, under the regime of General Secretary Brezhnev, General Grigorenko became disillusioned with the trend toward a return of Stalinism. He joined other dissidents who were speaking out against the growing repressions. Because of his World War II fame and his proven competence in the postwar years, he was placed in a psychiatric ward rather than a forced labor camp. His 1959 book is a collective work by faculty members of the Frunze Military Academy. *Methods of Military-Scientific Research* was a forerunner of the many books later published throughout the 1960s and 1970s about war-gaming and the need for scientific research in the military sphere. Readers of this work may be surprised to find both Stalin and Mao quoted as authorities.

4

Soviet Books and Pamphlets
on Military Doctrine and Strategy, 1960 to 1974

1960

According to some sources, a series of classified papers was prepared in 1960 to implement the new doctrine that Khrushchev had announced in his January 14, 1960, speech. Since the military doctrine was not openly explained during the course of the year, Soviet spokesmen throughout 1960 published relatively few military theoretical writings. This was a time of uncertainty for the Western student of Soviet military affairs.

1. Khrushchev, N. S., "Disarmament—The Way to a Sure Peace and Friendship Between Peoples." A speech delivered at the Fourth Session of the Supreme Soviet of the USSR. Published in *On Peaceful Coexistence* in English by Gospolitizdat, Moscow, 1960, 336 pages. The Soviet leader emphasizes the nuclear rocket strength of the Soviet armed forces, and downplays conventional weapons. This important speech is most worthwhile to study in light of changes that took place within the Soviet armed forces in the years that followed.

2. Ivanov, A. I. and Rybkin, G. I., *The Destructive Action of Nuclear Explosives* (Porazhayuscheye Deystviye Yadernovo Vzryva), Voyenizdat, 1960, 384 pages. This is a Soviet "popular science library" work, intended for a wide readership. The data on nuclear weapons are almost entirely from US sources. The authors quote Khrushchev's speech of January 14, 1960. Further references to this speech are seen again and again over the following decade.

3. Smirnov, M. V., General Major, Candidate of Military Science, Baz', I. S., Colonel, Kozlov, S. N., Colonel, and Sidorov, P. A., Colonel, *On Soviet Military Science* (O Sovetskoy Voyennoy Nauke), Voyenizdat, 1960, 336 pages. In the frontispiece, the publisher notes that all questions of military science are not settled, and that there is a need for further scientific work "with consideration of the development of military equipment and all of military affairs, and also with the rapid changes in contemporary armed struggle." This book, printed shortly after Khrushchev's speech announcing the new doctrine, states that rocket troops now "appear as the main service of the armed forces." The work is one of the transitional writings, written before the main questions concerning military science had been formulated.

4. Turchenko, V. V., Colonel, Candidate of Military Sciences, *Consolidation of Success in Battle* (Zakrepleniye Uspekha v Boyu), Voyenizdat, 1960, 128 pages. The purpose of the book is to examine questions of organization, and the conduct of combat actions of battalions, companies, and squads. It professes to analyze the character and peculiarities of contemporary battle. The work is intended for officers and sergeants of the various branches. One final page appears to have been added to this work to acknowledge the importance of nuclear weapons.

5. Grudinin, I. A., Colonel, Candidate of Philosophical Sciences. *Questions of Dialectics in Military Affairs* (Voprosy Dialektiki v Voyennom Dele), Voyenizdat, 1960, 216 pages. Colonel Grudinin later became a Doctor of Philosophical Sciences and remained one of the most articulate of Soviet military spokesmen throughout the 1960s. His last work, *Dialectics in Contemporary Military Affairs*, was published in 1971, shortly after his death in that year. This 1960 work was intended for officers of the Soviet Army and Navy. He does not at this time develop the theme of the new doctrine that had recently been announced by Khrushchev. The work is of particular interest when it is compared with his later writings.

6. Osilov, Z. S., General Major, *To New Heights of Party-Political Work in the Soviet Army and Navy* (K Novomu Pod'yemu Partiyno-Politicheskoy Raboty v Sovetskoy Armii i Flote), Voyenizdat, 1960,

376 pages. This book consists of speeches and articles by senior Soviet military officers, starting with the Minister of Defense, Marshal Malinovskiy. In the lead article, Malinovskiy directs specific attention to the nuclear-rocket weapon. The new doctrine is reflected in this publication.

7. Semenov, V. A. General Major (Reserve). *A Short Sketch of the Development of Soviet Operational Art* (Kratkiy Ocherk Razvitiya Sovetskovo Operativnovo Iskusstva), Voyenizdat, 1960, 300 pages. This book was given to the publisher in May 1959, and approval for final printing was given in February 1960. Its contents, in comparison with military theoretical writings printed two to five years later, appear very dated. No acknowledgment is made of Khrushchev's January speech. Nuclear weapons are mentioned, but they are not referred to as the decisive weapons.

8. Voropayev, D. A., Colonel, Candidate of Historical Science and Iovlev, A. M., Colonel, Candidate of Historical Sciences, *The Struggle of the CPSU in Creating Military Cadres* (Bor'ba KPSS Za Sozdaniye Voyennykh Kadrov), Voyenizdat, 1960, 244 pages. Mobilization in the Soviet armed forces is based on the cadre system. This book is largely historical in nature, but of interest because it comes at the very beginning of the major transformations that were starting in the structure of the Soviet armed forces.

1961

As previously noted, work was under way in the Soviet Union throughout 1960 concerning the problem of relating military science to the new doctrine. A few books did give some indications that major changes in military policies were taking place. The best explanations of Soviet military thought were given in two speeches, one by Party Chairman Khrushchev and the other by his Minister of Defense, Marshal Malinovsky.

1. Khrushchev, N. K., "For New Victories of the World Communist Movement," a speech delivered at a meeting of Representatives

of the Communist and Workers Movement, January 6, 1961. Published in *Communism—Peace and Happiness for the People*, Foreign Languages Publishing House, Moscow, 1963, pp. 28-43. Khrushchev repeated his theme of the military power of the Soviet Union, and talked about "how to prevent a world nuclear war." He called for "a time of Socialist revolutions and national-liberation revolutions." He attempted to define the various possible types of wars, and stated that "a small-scale imperialist war, no matter which of the imperialists may start it, may develop into a world thermonuclear missile war."

2. Malinovskiy, Rodion Ya., Marshal of the Soviet Union, Minister of Defense, "Speech of Comrade Malinovskiy, R. Ya," *22nd Congress of the Communist Party of the Soviet Union, Stenographic Notes* (22 S'Yezd Kommunisticheskoy Partii Sovetskovo Soyuza—Stenograficheskiy Otchet, vol. 2, p. 108), Gospolitizat, Moscow, 1962, pp. 108-128. In this speech to the 22nd Party Congress in October 1961, Malinovskiy expands on the doctrine previously announced by Khrushchev in January 1960. He states.

> The fundamental concrete tasks of the Armed Forces and the direction of military structuring in our country in present-day circumstances was distinctly and expressively laid down by our Supreme Commander-in-chief Nikita Sergeyevich Khrushchev in his historical speech at the Fourth Session of the Supreme Soviet of the USSR in 1960. In this report, a deep analysis of the nature of modern war, which lies at the base of Soviet military doctrine, was given.

With this acknowledgment, Malinovskiy proceeds to explain the nature of this new doctrine in greater detail.

3. Fedorov, G. A., Colonel, editor, *Marxism-Leninism on War and the Army* (Marksizm-Leninizm o Voyne i Armii), Voyenizdat, 1961, 24,000 copies, 396 pages. This book was prepared by a group of authors, consisting of faculty members of the Lenin Military-Political Academy. The book takes into account the "revolution in military affairs," and cites the January 1960 speech made by Party

Chairman Khrushchev. This book is well worth reviewing, especially for checking as to whether it agrees in basic concepts with *Military Strategy*, which appeared the following year. It is also useful to compare this work with later editions of *Marxism-Leninism on War and the Army*, published in 1964 and 1968.

4. *The Law of Life of a Soldier; A Collection of Articles* (Zakon Zhizni Voina: Sbornik Statey), Voyenizdat, 1961, 88 pages. This collection of articles appears as one of the first efforts to explain the implications of the new doctrine. The opening article, by Marshal of the Soviet Union A. A. Grechko, entitled "New Regulations for the Soviet Armed Forces," specifically refers to the January 14, 1960, speech made by Khrushchev. Articles by other senior Soviet military leaders dwell on the changes that were taking place in the Soviet Armed Forces.

5. *Program of the Communist Party of the Soviet Union: 22nd Party Congress* (Programma Kommunisticheskoy Partii Sovetskovo Soyuza), Pravda Publishing House, Moscow, 1961, 5,000,000 copies, 144 pages. This work gives the aspirations of the 22nd Party Congress in many different areas. One section, pages 110-112, is on the subject of "strengthening the armed forces and the military preparations of the Soviet Union." The book suggests the interest of the Party in the adequacy of its armed forces.

6. Konyukhovskiy, V. N., Colonel, Docent, Candidate of Historical Sciences, *The Territorial System of Military Construction* (Territorial'naya Sistema Voyennovo Stroitel'stva), Voyenizdat, 1961, 9,000 copies, 88 pages. In his January 1960 speech, Khrushchev appeared in favor of a territorial system for organizing the Soviet Army. This idea, however, was never implemented. Such a system is advanced in this pamphlet, which had been sent to the printers in 1960. It is interesting to read the author's advocacy of the system, especially in view of the later development of the Soviet Armed Forces.

7. Lagovskiy A. N., General Major, Doctor of Military Sciences, *Strategy and Economics* (Strategiya i Ekonomika), Voyenizdat,

1961, 7,500 copies, 264 pages. Much of this work is historical. The author does note the appearance of nuclear weapons, and how they have changed tactics, operational art, and strategy. On the other hand, he never actually relates the impact of nuclear weapons to his basic thesis on strategy and economics.

1962

This year marked the publication of two military works that remained as basic references for the remainder of the 1960s. The first was *Military Strategy*, edited by Marshal Sokolovskiy, and the second is a pamphlet, *Vigilantly Stand Guard Over the Peace*, by the Minister of Defense, Marshal Malinovskiy. The military doctrine announced by Khrushchev in 1960 has now had its impact upon military strategy and the Soviet Armed Forces as a whole.

1. Sokolovskiy, V. D., Marshal of the Soviet Union, editor, *Military Strategy* (Voyennaya Strategiya), Voyenizdat, 20,000 copies, 459 pages. This book appears to represent the findings of a group of Soviet officers assigned in 1960 to study the impact of nuclear weapons on warfare. It is the most significant work published by the Soviet authorities on military strategy in the past 50 years. Analysts may find it most useful to compare the first edition with subsequent editions, which appeared in 1963 and 1968. This book has been translated into English, and for years was the only major Soviet military-theoretical writing available to many US analysts.

2. Malinovskiy, R. Ya., Marshal of the Soviet Union, Minister of Defense, *Vigilantly Stand Guard Over the Peace* (Bditel'no Stoyat' Na Strazhe Mira), Voyenizdat, 100,000 copies, 72 pages. By coincidence, *Military Strategy* had appeared in Moscow bookstores approximately two months prior to the Cuban missile confrontation. This famed pamphlet by the Minister of Defense appeared approximately two months after the crisis. Specific mention is made of Cuba in the pamphlet. Malinovskiy further explains the impact of new weaponry upon the conduct of war. It is useful to compare this work with the basic concepts outlined in *Military Strategy*.

3. Trifonenkov, P. I., Colonel, Docent, Candidate of Philosophical Sciences, *On the Basic Laws of the Conduct and Outcome of Contemporary War* (Ob Osnovnykh Zakonakh Khoda i Iskhoda Sovremennoy Voyny), Voyenizdat, 1962, 8,000 copies, 120 pages. The work "is intended for officers, generals, and admirals." It is one of the few controversial Soviet books, and represents the author's own point of view. Nuclear weaponry receives main attention. This book, written by a "Candidate of Philosophical Sciences," should be compared with *Military Strategy*, which was written primarily by line officers, a few of whom had advanced degrees in military science.

4. Tyushkevich, S. A., Colonel, Candidate of Philosophical Sciences, *Necessity and Chance in War* (Neobkhodimost' i Sluchaynost' v Voyne), Voyenizdat, 1962, 11,500 copies, 136 pages. The author is primarily concerned with dialectics, as related to necessity and chance. It is interesting to see how he considers the "chance" start of a nuclear war. Like the work by Colonel Trifonenkov, given above, this work by Tyushkevich marks one of the early efforts to explain nuclear warfare in Marxist-Leninist terms.

5. *The Fundamentals of Soviet Military Legislation* (Osnovy Sovetskovo Voyennovo Zakonodatel'stva), Voyenizdat, 1962, 352 pages. This is a textbook for officers of the Soviet Army and Navy, prepared by the Lenin Military-Political Academy. It lists service obligations, legal standards, and rights of members of the Soviet Armed Forces. This book can be compared with the revisions made in Soviet military legislation in 1967, as given in *The Law of the USSR Regarding Universal Military Obligations*. Books such as this, while not dealing with doctrine and strategy, are useful for the analyst to read occasionally in order to have a more rounded appreciation of the Soviet Armed Forces.

6. Kuusinen, O. V., editor, *The Fundamentals of Marxism-Leninism* (Osnovy Marksizma-Leninizma), Political Literature Publishing House, Moscow, 1962, 400,000 copies, 784 pages. Practically every writing on Soviet military doctrine and strategy refers to the "principles of Marxism-Leninism." It is difficult, if not impossible, to understand Soviet foreign policy, military affairs, or negotiations at

SALT without some appreciation of this subject. This book on Marxism-Leninism has been translated into English. Dr. Georgiy A. Arbatov, present head of the Institute of the USA in Moscow and a frequent visitor to the United States, was one of the major contributors to this work.

1963

Following the Cuban missile confrontation in October 1962, there appeared to be a restudy by the Soviet leadership of certain matters of military science. For this reason, perhaps, relatively few significant military-theoretical works appeared in 1963. There were a sufficient number, however, to indicate the continuity of Soviet military thought.

1. Sokolovskiy, V. D., Marshal of the Soviet Union, editor, *Military Strategy* (Voyennaya Strategiya), Voyenizdat, 40,000 copies, 504 pages, 2nd edition. Interestingly, this work actually was changed but little from the 1962 edition. The list of contributors was virtually the same. (The 1968 edition of this work has been translated, and shows the additions and deletions of both the 1963 and 1968 versions.)

2. Krupnov, S. I., Colonel, Candidate of Philosophical Sciences, *Dialectics and Military Science* (Dialektika i Voyennaya Nauka), Voyenizdat, 1963, 9,500 copies, 205 pages. The book is "intended for generals and officers in the Soviet Army and Navy and also for commanders, engineers, and political workers." Colonel Krupnov, on the faculty of the Lenin Military-Political Academy, received his Doctorate in Philosophical Sciences in the early 1970s. At the time of writing, he appeared fully conversant with the direction Soviet military thought was to take, and he has done an excellent job in explaining the doctrinal decisions already made in Marxist-Leninist terms.

3. Rotmistrov, P. A., Chief Marshal of the Armored Forces, Doctor of Military Sciences, Professor, *The History of Military Art*

(Istoriya Voyennovo Iskusstva), Voyenizdat, 1963, vol. 1, 528 pages, vol. 2, 720 pages, 8,000 copies. This two-volume series was compiled by a group of authors assigned to the Department of the History of War and of Military Science at the Academy of the Tank Troops with Marshal Rotmistrov as editor. The work is intended "for officers and generals, also for military and civilian historians." These books cover the history of military art through 1945, and are well illustrated with maps. On the very last page, Rotmistrov recognizes the importance of nuclear weapons, but states that the new concepts will not invalidate the lessons of the past war.

1964

During this year, books written in the aftermath of the Cuban missile confrontation were beginning to appear in Moscow bookstores. Students of Soviet military matters might wonder whether or not Soviet military doctrine and strategy would change as a result of the nuclear test-ban agreements which were signed in Moscow in 1963. A series of books published in 1964 carried the same guidelines established in 1960.

1. Kozlov, S. N., General Major, Smirnov, M. V., General Major, Baz', I. S., Colonel. Sidorov, P. A., Colonel, *On Soviet Military Science* (O Sovetskoy Voyennoy Nauke), Voyenizdat, 1964, 15,000 copies, 406 pages. This is a very frank and well-written book, and its statements leave little room for misunderstanding. Soviet military doctrine and strategy are discussed at some length.

2. Popov, M. V., Colonel, Candidate of Philosophical Sciences, *The Essence of the Laws of Armed Combat* (Sushchnost' Zakonov Vooruzhennoy Bor'by), Voyenizdat, 1964, 7,000 copies, 138 pages. The work was prepared under the direction of Professor General Colonel N. A. Lomov, who at the time was at the General Staff Academy. It "is intended for officers, generals, and admirals of the Soviet Armed Forces, and also for all interested in philosophical problems of contemporary war and military science." This work is referenced in other Soviet military theoretical writings. It is listed in the 1968 *Calendar of a Soldier* as recommended reading.

3. Astashenkov, P. T., Colonel-Engineer, *Soviet Rocket Troops* (Sovetskiye Raketnyye Voyska), Voyenizdat, 1964, 30,000 copies, 236 pages, edited by General Colonel Tolubko, Deputy Chief, Strategic Rocket Troops. This book appeared shortly before Khrushchev's ouster. It gives a very frank discussion of the Soviet view of the nature of a future war, and the role of the strategic nuclear missile. The work can be compared with the 1967 edition, which appeared in the Brezhnev period, by the same author and with General Tolubko also listed as the editor.

4. Tsvetkov, G. G., Candidate of Psychological Sciences, Docent, editor, *On the Military-Theoretical Inheritance from V. I. Lenin* (O Voyenno-Teoreticheskom Nasledii V. I. Lenina), Voyenizdat, 1964, 20,000 copies, 288 pages. One chapter is by the well-known Colonel Ye. I. Rybkin. The book discusses both Soviet military science and military art.

5. Seleznev, I. A., Colonel, Candidate of Philosophical Sciences, *War and the Ideological Struggle* (Voyna i Ideologicheskaya Bor'ba), Voyenizdat, 7,000 copies, 340 pages. "The book is written for officers and generals studying the problems of nuclear rocket war and military science." An excellent summary of Soviet military doctrine is given on pp. 88-90.

6. Barabanshchikov, A. V., Lieutenant Colonel, Candidate of Pedagogical Sciences, editor, *The Basis of Military Teaching and Psychology* (Osnovy Voyennoy Pedagogiki i Psikhologii), Voyenizdat, 1964, 38,000 copies, 384 pages. The general theme of this work is the psychological conditioning of the Soviet Armed Forces for nuclear rocket warfare.

7. Grechko, A. A., Marshal of the Soviet Union, editor, *The Nuclear Age and War: A Military Survey* (Yadernyy Vek i Voyna: Voyennyye Obozreniya), Izvestia Publishing House, 1964, 100,000 copies, 160 pages. This work consists of a group of articles written by a number of very senior Soviet officers. It went to press July 15, 1964, shortly before Khrushchev was removed from power.

8. Krasil'nikov, S. N., General Lieutenant, Professor, Doctor of Military Sciences, editor, *The Atom and Weapons: Scientific-Tech-*

nical Progress and Military Affairs (Atom i Oruzhiye: Nauchno-Tekhnicheskiy Progress i Voyennoye Delo), Voyenizdat, 1964, 10,000 copies, 344 pages. This is a very basic and interesting book showing the development of technology and its relationship to each of the Soviet miltary services. Much of the technical data is from the US press.

1965

A series of major military works was published during this year, almost all of which must have been started under Khrushchev's regime. By the time they were published, references to him had been completely removed. The political-military authorities wanted to ensure that all members of the Soviet Armed Forces thoroughly understood the revolution in military affairs that was so radically changing the Armed Forces.

1. Derevyanko, P. M., editor, *Problems of the Revolution in Military Affairs* (Problemy Revolyutsii v Voyennom Dele), Voyenizdat, 1965, 16,000 copies, 196 pages. Almost all of the articles in this work had previously been published in *Red Star* or *Communist of the Armed Forces* while Khrushchev was in power. They have been carefully reedited to delete all mention of him. The book actually was submitted to the printers on October 24, 1964, two weeks after the Khrushchev ouster. It appeared in Moscow bookstores early in 1965. Marshal Malinovskiy's article, "The Revolution in Military Affairs and the Tasks of the Military Writer," is the first in the book. Other contributors were General Colonel Shtemenko, now Chief of Staff, Warsaw Pact Forces, and General Lieutenant of Aviation N. A. Sbytov, Candidate of Military Sciences, who succeeded General Lomov at the General Staff Academy. This book is recommended in the *Calendar of a Soldier*.

2. Sushko, N. Ya, General Major and Tyushkevich, S. A., Colonel, editors, *Marxism-Leninism on War and the Army* (Marksizm-Leninizm o Voyne i Armii), Voyenizdat, 1965, 50,000 copies, 384 pages, 4th edition. This work presents an excellent discussion of the

Soviet Party-military view of the nature of a future war. The book was nominated for a Frunze Prize in 1966, and is listed in *Bolshaya Encyclopedia* as a basic reference in military doctrine. It is one of the "Officer's Library" series.

3. Zav'yalov, I. G., General Major, *Speed, Time and Space in Contemporary War* (Skorost', Vremya i Prostranstvo v Sovremennoy Voyne), Voyenizdat 1965, 8,000 copies, 192 pages. This work "is of practical interest for military readers, especially for generals, admirals, and officers of the Soviet Armed Forces." General Zav'yalov is one of the contributors to all three editions of *Military Strategy* and, judging by his published works, is a highly authoritative spokesman. Recommended in *Calendar of a Soldier.*

4. Bochkarev, K. S., General Major, editor, *Program of the CPSU on the Defense of the Socialist Fatherland* (Programma KPSS o Zashchite Sotsialisticheskovo Otechestva), Voyenizdat, 1965, 22,000 copies, 176 pages. A valuable book. The following subheadings are of particular interest: "On the Character and Types of War in the Present Period," pp. 29-42; and "The Contemporary Revolution in Military Affairs and Its Significance," pp. 83-110. Listed as recommended reading in the *Calendar of a Soldier.*

5. Radziyevskiy, A. I., General Colonel, Professor, editor, *Dictionary of Basic Military Terms* (Slovar' Osnovnykh Voyennykh Terminov), Voyenizdat, 1965, 27,000 copies, 248 pages. Compiled by a group of authors under the direction of the faculty of the General Staff Academy, this work is intended for "officers, generals, and admirals of all services." An important work which can be used in conjunction with the *Explanatory Directory of Military Terms*, issued in 1966. An "Officer's Library" publication, and on the *Calendar of a Soldier* recommended list.

6. Prokop'yev, N.P., *On War and the Army: A Short Sketch* (O Voyne i Armii: Kratkiy Ocherk), Voyenizdat, 1965, 13,000 copies, 296 pages. The book is intended for young officers studying Marxist-Leninist theory on war and the Army. Changes brought about by the

revolution in military affairs are discussed. The author's view of Soviet military science is most interesting.

7. Zubarev, G. A., *Cooperation of Troops in Combined Arms Battle* (Vzaimodeystviye Voysk v Obshchevoyskovom Boyu), Voyenizdat, 1965, 7,000 copies, 152 pages. A work prepared for Soviet Ground Forces officers, students of military schools, kursants, and others. It reflects the impact of nuclear weapons upon ground warfare.

8. *Organization and Armaments of the Armies and Navies of Capitalist Governments* (Organizatsiya i Vooruzheniye Armiy i Flotov Kapitalisticheskikh Gosudarstv), Voyenizdat, 1965, 30,000 copies, 548 pages. A collective work. The Soviet reader can obtain much more data from this book about foreign contemporary weapon systems than he can from his own forces. In general, Soviet readers are much better informed on foreign armies than the US reader is on the Soviet Armed Forces. This is an "Officer's Library" book, and recommended in *Calendar of a Soldier*.

9. Mamay, N. P., Candidate of Historical Sciences, *V. I. Lenin on War, the Army and Military Science* (V. I. Lenin o Voyne, Armii i Voyennoy Nauke), Voyenizdat, 1965, 29,000 copies, 836 pages. This work consists of a collection of articles. It is one of the "Officer's Library" series, is given as a reference in the *Bolshaya Encyclopedia*, and listed as recommended reading in *Calendar of a Soldier*.

10. *M. V. Frunze: Selected Works* (M. V. Frunze: Izbrannyye Proizvedeniya), Voyenizdat, 1965, 27,000 copies, 528 pages. This is the first book printed in the "Officer's Library" series. It is often quoted as a basic source of Soviet military thought and organization. It consists entirely of articles by M. V. Frunze.

11. Slukhay, I. A., Colonel, *Rockets and Tradition* (Rakety i Traditsii), Voyenizdat, 1965, 18,000 copies, 224 pages. This work is intended for popular readership. It is very basic, and of interest in that it discusses the introduction of rockets into all of the Soviet services. The author briefly notes how the revolution in military affairs has changed the nature of armies.

12. Bulatov, A. A., and Prozorov, V. G., *Tactical Surprise* (Takti-cheskaya Vnezapnost'), Voyenizdat, 1965, 5,500 copies, 168 pages. The book is intended for a wide circle of military readers. A number of examples are given on how to achieve tactical surprise. These examples are taken from the lessons of World War II. The authors note that with the appearance of nuclear weapons, the factor of sur-prise has increased; and surprise, combined with the use of nuclear weapons, might totally defeat the enemy in a short period of time.

13. Kadishev, A. B., Colonel (Retired), Doctor of Historical Sci-ences, *Problems of Strategy and Operational Art in Soviet Military Works, 1917-1940* (Voprosy Strategii i Operativnovo Iskusstva v Sovetskikh Voyennykh Trudakh), Voyenizdat, 1965, 6,500 copies, 768 pages. Contains a long introduction written by Marshal Zakha-rov, former Chief of the Soviet General Staff. The book contains selections from major Soviet military writers, beginning with M. V. Frunze. Many of the writings were withdrawn from general circula-tion during the Stalin regime. Approximately half of the authors listed died in Stalin's purges of 1937-38. It should be noted that in 1970 a companion book, *Problems of Tactics in Soviet Military Writings*, was also issued by Voyenizdat, and that both books were nominated for a Frunze Prize in 1973.

1966

The weapon systems that the Soviet Armed Forces have at their disposal in 1975 were in development or in initial production in 1966. It is interesting to see how Soviet military-political spokesmen treated doctrine, strategy, and the nature of future war at this time. These military publications could indicate the direction in which the Soviet Armed Forces were planning to go. The analyst should note that the 23rd Party Congress met in this year.

1. Sushko, N. Ya., General Major, Candidate of Philosophical Sciences, and Kondratkov, T. R., Lieutenant Colonel, Candidate of Philosophical Sciences, editors, *Methodological Problems of Military Theory and Practice* (Metodologicheskiye Problemy Voyennoy Teorii i Praktiki), Voyenizdat, 1966, 45,000 copies, 328 pages.

Among the contributors to this work were Lieutenant Colonel V. M. Bondarenko, Lieutenant Colonel V. G. Kozlov, General Major S. N. Kozlov, Colonel M. V. Popov, and General Major Ye. F. Sulimov. Almost all of these contributors possess advanced degrees in military sciences or in philosophical science. Of particular interest is the discussion of the revolution in military affairs. This work is listed as a reference in the *Bolshaya Encyclopedia,* and recommended reading in *Calendar of a Soldier.* It is most worthwhile to compare this edition with the second edition, which appeared in 1969.

2. Reznichenko, V. G., General Major, Candidate of Military Sciences, Docent, editor, *Tactics* (Taktika), Voyenizdat, 1966, 40,000 copies, 408 pages. Contributors to this work are on the staff of the Frunze Military Academy with advanced degrees in military science. The book shows the changes brought about in tactics as a result of the revolution in military affairs. The *Bolshaya Encyclopedia* lists this work as a reference, and the *Calendar of a Soldier* has it as recommended reading. It is one of the "Officer's Library" series, and was nominated for a Frunze Prize in 1968. It has been translated into English.

3. Strokov, A. A., Colonel, Doctor of Historical Sciences, Professor, *The History of Military Art* (Istoriya Voyennovo Iskusstva), Voyenizdat, 1966, 35,000 copies, 656 pages. The book consists of a number of articles written by officers of the Lenin Military-Political Academy and the Frunze Military Academy. The last two chapters of this book, pp. 587-639, deal with the post-World War II period, and provide a clear summary of Soviet military doctrine and strategy through 1965. This is an "Officer's Library" work which has been listed as a reference and is recommended reading in the *Bolshaya Encyclopedia,* the *Officer's Handbook,* and *Calendar of a Soldier.*

4. Skuybeda, P. I., Colonel, editor, *Explanatory Dictionary of Military Terms* (Tolkovyy Slovar' Voyennykh Terminov), Voyenizdat, 1966, 35,000 copies, 528 pages. This work contains approximately 2,000 terms, listed in alphabetical order. It is one of the most useful books ever published by the Soviet military press, and provides Soviet definitions of terms which may differ entirely from

US concepts. The *Calendar of a Soldier* includes it in its "Soldier's Bookshelf."

5. Semeyko, L. S., Colonel, Candidate of Military Science, *Foresight of a Commander in Battle* (Predvideniye Komandira v Boyu), Voyenizdat, 1966, 12,000 copies, 184 pages. This work is intended for officers and generals of the Soviet Army, and also for all interested in military-philosophical problems of contemporary battle. The book is "intended for discussion," and "reflects a certain point of view." In 1974, Colonel Semeyko was serving as a full-time member of the Institute of the USA. His work is listed as recommended reading in the *Calendar of a Soldier*.

6. Gornyy, A. A., General Lieutenant, Justice, editor, *Fundamentals of Soviet Military Legislation* (Osnovy Sovetskovo Voyennovo Zakonodatel'stva), Voyenizdat, 1966, 40,000 copies, 432 pages. The work is by a group of authors. It is intended as a textbook for officers attending higher military schools. This is one of the "Officer's Library" series of books, and recommended in the *Calendar of a Soldier*. While not concerned specifically with doctrine and strategy, it helps to provide an understanding of the Soviet Armed Forces.

7. Barabanshchikov, A. V., Lieutenant Colonel, Candidate of Pedagogical Sciences, Docent, editor, *Military Pedagogics* (Voyennaya Pedagogika), Voyenizdat, 1966, 40,000 copies, 376 pages. This work was compiled by members of the Lenin Military-Political Academy. It outlines the instructional methods that are to be used throughout the Soviet Armed Forces. The work is also one of the "Officer's Library" series, and is listed in the *Calendar of a Soldier*.

1967

In hindsight, especially when reviewing the provisions of SALT I and II, it becomes apparent that books published in 1967 provided an indication of the path the new power group that had disposed of Khrushchev intended to follow. The close Party-military tie is reflected in a number of the writings.

1. Zheltov, A. S., General Colonel, editor, *V. I. Lenin and the Soviet Armed Forces* (V. I. Lenin i Sovetskiye Vooruzhennyye Sily), Voyenizdat, 1967, 50,000 copies, 448 pages. General Colonel Zheltov is Head, Lenin Military-Political Academy. One of the other noted contributors was General Major A. A. Strokov, Department Head, Institute of Military History, Ministry of Defense. This work won a Frunze Prize in 1968, and is listed in *Calendar of a Soldier*. It is generally historical in nature, but pp. 225-227, 258, and 264 provide excellent statements of strategy, doctrine, and the nature of any future war.

2. Kiryayev, N. M., General Major, Doctor of Historical Sciences, Professor, *The CPSU and the Building of the Soviet Armed Forces* (KPSS i Stroitel'stvo Sovetskikh Vooruzhennykh Sil), Voyenizdat, 1967, 30,000 copies, 464 pages. The fourth section of the last chapter of the book is entitled, "The Development of Soviet Military Doctrine by the Communist Party." There also is a section entitled, "The Revolution in Military Affairs." This book is an *Officer's Handbook* recommendation, and is also included in the "Soldier's Bookshelf."

3. Astashenkov, P. T., Engineer-Colonel, *Soviet Rocket Troops* (Sovetskiye Raketnyye Voyska), Voyenizdat, 1967, 11,000 copies, 344 pages. The Introduction is by General Colonel Tolubko, then Deputy Chief of the Rocket Troops, who since has been appointed as CINC. This is a very frank account of Soviet aspirations in rockets and space. It is most useful to compare the contents of this work with the 1964 edition, published in the Khrushchev era. When the book appeared in 1967, copies were very difficult to obtain. For some reason that still is not clear, copies suddenly appeared on Moscow military bookshelves in 1971. This is a "popular science library" effort, and is listed as recommended reading both in the *Officer's Handbook* and the *Calendar of a Soldier*.

4. Dyachenko, M. I., Colonel, Docent, and Fedenko, N. F., Major, editors, *Military Psychology* (Voyennaya Psikhologiya), Voyenizdat, 1967, 50,000 copies, 260 pages. Written by a group of authors at the Lenin Military-Political Academy, the work examines the Pavlovian

method and its application to the conditioning of troops in conditions of nuclear rocket war. This is an "Officer's Library" publication, and is recommended in both the *Officer's Handbook* and *Calendar of a Soldier*. It is worth careful study.

5. Modrzhinskaya, Ye. D., Grigoryan, B. T., and Kondratkov, T. R., *Problems of War and Peace* (Problemy Voyny i Mira), Mysl' Publishing House, 1967, 7,500 copies. An excellent overview of Soviet concepts of types of war. Although not noted in the book, T. R. Kondratkov actually is a colonel and a well-known military-political spokesman. Another of the authors, A. N. Kalyadin, is on the staff of the Institute of World Economy and International Relations (IMEMO), and has visited the United States. This work has been translated into English by the Foreign Technological Division.

6. Zakharov, M. V., Marshal of the Soviet Union, Chief of the General Staff, *On the Scientific Approach to Troop Management* (O Nauchnam Podkhodye k Rukovodstvu Voyskami), Voyenizdat, 1967, 50,000 copies, 80 pages. The purpose of the book is "to help the officers of the Soviet Army and Navy have a deep understanding of the demands required of them by the revolution in military affairs." This book is given as recommended reading in the *Officer's Handbook*, listed in the *Bolshaya Encyclopedia* as a reference, and also included in the "Soldier's Bookshelf" section of a number of editions of *Calendar of a Soldier*.

7. Petrus', P. M., Shemanskiy, P. V., and Chul'sky, N. K., *Nuclear Weapons and the Development of Tactics* (Yadernoye Oruzhiye i Razvitiye Taktiki), Voyenizdat, 1967, 18,000 copies, 240 pages. This work is "intended for officers and generals of the Ground Forces of the Soviet Army." It is a very useful publication, and provides Soviet views of the role of the Ground Forces in nuclear war. It is included in the "Soldier's Bookshelf."

8. Piterskiy, N. A., Vice Admiral (Retired), Candidate of Naval Sciences, *The Combat Path of the Soviet Navy* (Boyevoy Put' Sovetskovo Voyenno-Morskovo Flota), Voyenizdat, 1967, 25,000 copies, 592 pages. Although generally historical in nature, the last

chapter of this book discusses postwar development of the Soviet Navy. An *Officer's Handbook* recommendation.

9. *To Be In Formation* (Yest' Stat' v Stroy), Young Guards Publishing House, Moscow, 1967, 100,000 copies, 256 pages. This work consists of a selection of articles by senior Soviet officers. Each explains the particular service to which he is assigned. These articles are excellent in reflecting the basic doctrine and strategy of the Soviet Armed Forces.

10. *The Law of the USSR Regarding Universal Military Obligations* (Zakon SSSR o Vseobshchey Voinskoy Obyazannosti), Voyenizdat, 1967, cost, 5 kopeks, 48 pages. Marshal Grechko's speech, given at the Third Session of the Supreme Soviet, Seventh Plenum, October 12, 1967, makes up the first article of this pamphlet. The text of the law on universal military service, passed at that session, is also included. Both the *Officer's Handbook* and the *Calendar of a Soldier* list this work as a basic reference.

11. Anureyev, I. I., General Major of the Engineer-Technical Services and Doctor of Military Science, Professor, and Tatarchenko, A. Ye., Engineer-Colonel, Docent, and Candidate of Military Sciences, *The Use of Mathematical Models in Military Affairs* (Primeneniye Matematicheskikh Metodov v Voyennom Dele), Voyenizdat, 1967, 244 pages. This is a very technical work. Chapters cover such subjects as the use of the theory of probability, the theory of games, and methods of mathematical programming in military affairs. The book is listed in the *Calendar of a Soldier*.

12. *M. I. Kalinin on Communist Ideology and Military Duty* (M. I. Kalinin o Kommunisticheskom Vospitanii i Voinskom Dolge), Voyenizdat, 1967, 32,000 copies, 728 pages. This lengthy book contains writings by Kalinin. It is one of the "Officer's Library" series.

1968

During the course of this year, a number of very significant military-theoretical writings appeared, which continued to be widely quoted and studied into the 1970s. Included in these are the following:

1. Sokolovskiy, V. D., Marshal of the Soviet Union, editor, *Military Strategy* (Voyennaya Strategiya), Voyenizdat, 1968, 30,000 copies, 464 pages, 3rd edition. In general, this work is by the same group of authors who published the first edition in 1962 and the second in 1963. The 1968 edition was nominated for a Frunze Prize in 1969, and is listed in both the *Officer's Handbook* and *Bolshaya Encyclopedia* as recommended reading. It is referenced in various editions of *Calendar of a Soldier*. The 1968 edition has been translated into English, with changes from the first and second editions clearly identified. This also is an "Officer's Library" book.

2. *50 Years of the Armed Forces of the USSR* (50 Let Vooruzhennykh Sil SSR), Voyenizdat, 1968, 100,000 copies, 584 pages. Like *Military Strategy*, this is one of the most authoritative military writings of the 1960s. It won a 1970 Frunze Prize, is listed as recommended reading in three of the chapters in the *Officers Handbook*, and is given as a basic reference at least three times in the 1971 *Bolshaya Encyclopedia*. The book was prepared by an editorial commission headed by the late Marshal Zakharov. Also on the commission were all of the CINCs, together with senior Marshals of the Soviet Union such as Konev and Sokolovskiy. The book traces the development of Soviet military doctrine and strategy through the postwar period.

3. Tyushkevich, S. A., Colonel, Candidate of Philosophical Sciences, Docent, Sushko, N. Ya, General Major (Retired), Candidate of Philosophical Sciences, Docent, *et al,* editors, *Marxism-Leninism on War and the Army*, (Marksizm-Leninizm o Voyne i Armii), Voyenizdat, 1968, 170,000 copies, 382 pages, 5th edition. The work is by a collective of authors, including many of the most noted Soviet political-military spokesmen, such Ye. I. Rybkin. The book is "intended for officers, generals, and admirals, studying Marxist-Leninist teachings on war and the Army." Of particular value is the fact that this edition can be compared with earlier editions, which were printed during the Khrushchev regime as well as immediately after his ouster. The discussion on military doctrine is most provocative. This is included in the "Soldier's Bookshelf."

4. Krasovskiy, S. A., Marshal of Aviation, editor, *Aviation and Cosmonautics of the USSR* (Aviatsiya i Kosmonavtika SSSR), Voyenizdat, 1968, 25,000 copies, 600 pages. This book represents a combined effort of contributors from the Soviet Air Force Academy, the research institutes of civil aviation, and with assistance from the Lenin Military-Political Academy and the staff of *Aviation and Cosmonautics*. Coverage of the postwar Soviet Air Force is brief, but includes the revolution in military affairs. This work is recommended reading in the *Officer's Handbook*, and was one of five books nominated for a Frunze Prize in 1970.

5. Sulimov, Ye. F., General Major, Professor, Doctor of Philosophical Sciences, editor, *The Basis of Scientific Communism* (Osnovy Nauchnovo Kommunizma), Voyenizdat, 1968, 200,000 copies, 528 pages. Contributors to the book are faculty members of the Lenin Military-Political Academy. Each of the higher military schools in the Soviet Union has a department of scientific communism. To understand Soviet military doctrine and strategy today, it is first necessary to have a basic appreciation of this subject. The work is recommended in *Calendar of a Soldier*.

6. Khmel', A. Ye., General Lieutenant, *Party-Political Work in the Soviet Armed Forces* (Partiyno-Politicheskaya Rabota v Sovetskikh Vooruzhennykh Silakh), Voyenizdat, 1968, 65,000 copies, 352 pages. This is the 14th book of the "Officer's Library" series. An abridged edition has been translated into English. This work should be read in its entirety. The book explains the control of the Party over the Soviet military, and provides an excellent discussion of Party-military relationships. Recommended in the *Officer's Handbook*.

7. Batitskiy, P. E., Marshal of the Soviet Union, editor, *The Troops of National PVO: A Historical Sketch* (Voyska Protivovozdushnoy Oborony Strany: Istoricheskiy Ocherk), Voyenizdat, 1968, 50,000 copies, 440 pages. This is a collective work. Although generally historical, there is some discussion of PVO in the postwar period. Of particular interest is the discussion of defenses against manned aircraft. The work is listed in *Calendar of a Soldier*.

8. Sokolov, P. V., Candidate of Economic Science, Docent, editor, *Military-Economic Problems in a Course on Political Econ-*

omy (Voyenno-Ekonomicheskiye Voprosy v Kursye Politekonomii), Voyenizdat, 1968, 40,000 copies, 304 pages. This book is to help students of military academies, evening students at Marxist-Leninist universities, and all interested in military-economic programs. The authors examine and compare, from the Soviet viewpoint, capitalist and Socialist military-economic systems. A *Calendar of a Soldier* listing.

9. Vysotskiy, V. K., Colonel, Quartermaster Service, Docent, and Candidate of Military Sciences, *The Rear Services of the Soviet Army* (Tyl Sovetskoy Armii), Voyenizdat, 1968, 20,000 copies, 320 pages. The work provides a short historical sketch of the formation of the Soviet Rear Services. The last chapter, "The Postwar Period, 1946-1967," gives a summary of current concepts. A *Calendar of a Soldier* recommendation.

10. Suzdalev, N. I., *Submarines Against Submarines* (Podvodnyye Lodki Protiv Podvodnykh Lodok), Voyenizdat, 1968, 10,500 copies, 164 pages. Most of the material is from the "foreign" press. The book is intended for personnel of the Army and Navy who are interested in naval themes. The usual claim is made about the US and its designs on the Soviet Union. This work reflects some possible Soviet concepts of submarine defense.

11. Nadirov, Yu. S., Velenets, I. S., Druzhinin, L. M., Pavlov, Ye. I., *The Defense of Subunits from Weapons of Mass Destruction* (Zashchita Podrazdeleniy ot Oruzhiya Massovovo Porazheniya), Voyenizdat, 1968, 100,000 copies, 224 pages. "Intended for commander of subunits of Ground Forces troops, kursants, and students in military schools, and for reserve officers," this work suggests Soviet concepts of the use of weapons of mass destruction, and how they would provide for the survival of their own forces. The book is general in nature, and does not deal with specifics.

12. Rogov, I. V., and Bol'shev, B.N., *Methods of Teaching the Material Parts of Tank Armaments* (Metodika Izucheniya Material-'noy Chasti Tankovovo Vooruzheniya), Voyenizdat, 1968, 12,000 copies, 152 pages. This book is for officers and sergeants of tank troops, and also for students at tank schools. The authors develop concepts of the role of tanks in nuclear warfare.

13. Petrov, Yu. P., Colonel, Doctor of Historical Sciences, Professor, *Building the Political Organs of the Party and the Komsomol Organizations of the Army and Navy* (Stroitel'stvo Politorganov, Partiynykh i Komsomol'skikh Organizatsiy Armii i Flota), Voyenizdat, 1968, 18,000 copies, 544 pages. This work shows Party-military relations within the military, and the role of the military-political schools. It is excellent work for obtaining a basic understanding of the Party's influence within the Soviet military. A *Calendar of a Soldier* listing.

14. *V. I. Lenin on the Defense of the Socialist Fatherland* (V. I. Lenin o Zashchite Sotsialisticheskovo Otechestva), Voyenizdat, 1968, 310,000 copies, 368 pages. This is a collection of articles asserting basic tenets of faith. It is an *Officer's Handbook* recommendation.

15. Safronov, I. V., General Lieutenant (Retired), editor, *Officer's Guide for Quartermasters* (Spravochnik Ofitsera Po Voyskovomu Khozyaystvu), Voyenizdat, 1968, 32,000 copies, 272 pages. This is a basic work "for commanders and political workers in units and subunits of all the services of the Soviet Army and Navy." It also is intended for students and kursants of military schools. The frontispiece suggests that it would also be useful for workers in the Rear Services and for finance officers, and that it should be placed in clubs and libraries. This is one of the "Officer's Library" series, and gives interesting insights into the functioning of the Soviet Armed Forces.

1969

The usual three or four significant books on military-theoretical subjects appeared in 1969. As will be shown, two were new editions of previous books, and provided the analyst with an excellent opportunity to compare where, if at all, a shift in Soviet military thought had taken place.

1. Zheltov, A. S., General Colonel, Commandant of the Lenin Military-Political Academy, editor, *Methodological Problems of Military Theory and Practice* (Metodologicheskiye Problemy Voyennoy

Teorii i Praktiki), Voyenizdat, 1969, 60,000 copies, 512 pages, 2nd edition. The first edition of this book appeared in 1966, with Lieutenant Colonel Kondratkov as editor. Contributing editors to the 1969 edition were Colonel Bondarenko, General Major Sushko, General Major Kozlov, and other noted political-military spokesmen. This book discusses doctrine and strategy in the nuclear age. It was listed two times in the 1971 *Officer's Handbook* as recommended reading, and was also referenced in the 1971 *Bolshaya Encyclopedia*. It is a major work. Nominated for a Frunze Prize in 1970.

2. Zheltov, A. S., General Colonel, editor, *V. I. Lenin and the Soviet Armed Forces* (V. I. Lenin i Sovetskiye Vooruzhennyye Sily), Voyenizdat, 1969, 100,000 copies, 416 pages, 2nd edition. The first edition of this work appeared in 1966, by essentially the same group of authors. Many of the key issues of the day affecting the Soviet Armed Forces are mentioned, from military doctrine to military superiority. This work appears to be considered authoritative by the Soviets, since it is listed at the end of three chapters of the *Officers' Handbook* as recommended reading, and also given as a reference in the 1971 *Bolshaya Encyclopedia*. It is included in *Calendar of a Soldier*.

3. Lototskiy, S. S., *Army of the Soviets* (Armiya Sovetskaya), Politizdat (Political Publishing House), 1969, 100,000 copies, 446 pages. For some reason, the publishers do not state that the author is a General Lieutenant, who heads the Department of History and of Military Art at the Frunze Military Academy. In 1971, the Foreign Languages Publishing House printed an English edition of this work. Most of the work is historical; the last section, entitled "Safeguarding the Peace," discusses the revolution in military affairs and the basic tenets of Soviet military doctrine.

4. Chernenko, K. U., and Savinkin, N. I., editors, *The CPSU on the Armed Forces of the Soviet Union* (KPSS o Vooruzhennykh Silakh Sovetskovo Soyuza), Voyenizdat, 1969, 100,000 copies, 472 pages. This collection of documents, speeches, and declarations covers the period 1917 to 1968. It is an excellent reference work, and is listed in the 1971 *Officer's Handbook* as recommended reading.

5. Buzunov, V. K., Docent, Candidate of Military Sciences, *The Aerodrome: The Fighting Position of Aviation* (Aerodrom: Boevaya Positsiya Aviatsii), (The Aviation-Technical Supply of Aviation), Voyenizdat, 1969, 7,500 copies, 128 pages. Much of this material is from the US press. Some Soviet concepts of supporting aircraft are also given.

6. Bokaryev, V. A., Engineer Colonel, Docent, Candidate of Philosophical Sciences, *Cybernetics and Military Affairs* (Kibernetika i Voyennoye Delo), Voyenizdat, 1968, 13,000 copies, 288 pages. The author examines cybernetics from a philosophical basis and for its use in modeling. In the latter part of the work, he discusses the use of cybernetics in warfare, in aiding military preparedness, and in directing troops. This is a *Calendar of a Soldier* recommendation.

7. Kurochkin, P. A., General of the Army, Professor, editor, *Basic Methods of Military-Scientific Research* (Osnovy Metodiki Voyenno-Nauchnovo Issledovaniya), Voyenizdat, 1968, 5,600 copies, 248 pages. A collection of articles by the faculty of the Frunze Military Academy. It is intended for officers doing their first studies in science and students at higher military educational institutions. It is a fairly basic book, describing the fundamentals of research placed in a Marxist-Leninist mold.

8. Lyutov, I. S., Colonel, and Sagaydak, P. T., Colonel, *The Motorized Rifle Battalion in a Tactical Airborne Landing* (Moto-strelkovyy Batal'on v Takticheskom Vozdushnom Desante), Voyenizdat, 1969, 8,000 copies, 176 pages. This work is intended for officers of motorized infantry units and for students attending military schools. It is of interest in its treatment of nuclear and nonnuclear combat conditions.

9. Lashchenko, P. N., General of the Army, *The Style of the Work of the Commander* (Stil' Raboty Komandira), Voyenizdat, 1969, 26,000 copies, 248 pages. An informal work in which the author, a very senior commander, gives his experiences and personal techniques of command. He notes how "the revolution in military affairs" raised the requirements of officers. The work is included in the "Soldier's Bookshelf."

10. Il'yin, S. K., General Major, *The Moral Factor in Contemporary War* (Moral'nyy Faktor v Sovremenoy Voyne), Voyenizdat, 1969, 40,000 copies, 176 pages. The author, on the editorial board of *Military Herald*, stresses the superiority of the Communist social system over "imperialism," and describes the necessity for the moral-political and psychological preparation of troops. This is another work included in the "Soldier's Bookshelf."

11. Isakov, P. F., Colonel, editor, *The Work of the Komsomols in the Soviet Army and Navy* (Komsomol'skaya Rabota v Sovetskoy Armii i Flote), by a group of authors, Voyenizdat, 1968, 50,000 copies, 216 pages. Intended for students of higher Party schools and for a "wide circle" of other readers, this work describes the activities of the Communist Party in the Soviet Armed Forces. It shows the absolute control maintained over all aspects of the soldier's life.

12. Gastilovich, A. I., General Colonel, Doctor of Military Sciences, *Journey of a Soldier* (Put' Soldata), DOSAAF Publishing House, Moscow, 1969, 100,000 copies, 80 pages. This pamphlet gives the life story of one of the Soviet officers largely responsible for developing Soviet military doctrine and strategy during the late 1950s and early 1960s, General Colonel A. I. Gastilovich. Chapter seven in all three editions of *Military Strategy* is specifically attributed to this officer, and is the only portion of the book in which the author is identified. The *Penkovskiy Papers* speak of the "Special Collection," a group of Top Secret papers which discuss the problems of a future war and the new Soviet military doctrine. According to Penkovskiy, "the theme for the entire series was set by Lieutenant General Gastilovich in his article, 'The Theory of Military Art Needs Review.'" *Journey of a Soldier* is of interest in that it describes the military career of one of the most influential of Soviet strategists.

1970

Books published in 1970 continued to be of interest, and half a dozen were concerned with questions of doctrine and strategy. Two books also reported on two previous military exercises. Among the works of direct or indirect interest to the student of Soviet military affairs are the following:

1. Sidorenko, A. A., Colonel, Candidate of Military Sciences, *The Offensive* (Nastupleniye), Voyenizdat, 1970, 13,000 copies, 232 pages. The book is intended for officers of the Soviet Army, students at military-educational institutions, and reserve officers. This work is a "calculation of the experience of past wars, uncovering the character of the attack and especially its conduct, including the use of the nuclear weapon and destructive firepower, the methods of crushing the defenses of the enemy and achieving success." It also includes "questions of the pursuit, and of forcing military obstacles and night attack." Recommended in *Calendar of a Soldier*, 1972.

2. Skirdo, M. P., Colonel, Doctor of Philosophical Sciences, Professor, *The People, the Army and the General* (Narod, Armiya, Polkovodets), Voyenizdat, 1970, 16,500 copies, 208 pages. This work "examines the characteristic features of contemporary war." The book "will undoubtedly catch the interest of officers and generals. It may also be recommended for students of higher military institutions, and evening students of universities of Marxism-Leninism." Despite the theoretical sound of this book, it nevertheless deals with the usual concepts of the Soviet view of warfare in the nuclear-rocket age. Also listed as recommended reading in the 1972 *Calendar of a Soldier*.

3. Lomov, N. A., General Colonel, Professor, *Scientific-Technical Progress and the Development of Military Affairs* (Nauchno-Tekhnicheskiy Progress i Razvitiye Voyennovo Dela), Nauka Publishing House (the publishing house of the Academy of Sciences), 1970, 10,000 copies, 48 pages. General Colonel Lomov formerly was a senior professor at the General Staff Academy. At the time of the publication of this work, he was a consultant at the Institute of the USA. Since the Institute comes under the Academy of Sciences, it was perhaps for this reason that their publishing house issued the pamphlet. General Lomov discusses doctrine, the revolution in military affairs, and the role of strategic nuclear forces.

4. Zakharov, M. V., Marshal of the Soviet Union, Chief of the General Staff, editor, *V. I. Lenin and Military History* (V. I. Lenin i

Voyennaya Istoriya), Voyenizdat, 1970, 10,000 copies, 324 pages. This book gives the findings of a conference held in June 1969 at the Institute of Military History, Ministry of Defense. Participants were from the General Staff and the Lenin Military-Political Academy. The work contains articles by well-known individuals such as General Lieutenant Zhilin, Head of the Soviet Military History Department, General Colonel N. A. Lomov, and General Major Ye. F. Sulimov, three very articulate Soviet military writers.

5. Kadishev, A. B., Colonel (Retired), Doctor of Historical Sciences, editor, *Problems of Tactics in Soviet Military Works: 1917-1940* (Voprosy Taktiki v Sovetskikh Voyennykh Trudakh), Voyenizdat, 1970, 8,000 copies, 520 pages. A book "for generals, admirals, and officers of the Soviet Armed Forces, and may be used as a textbook for students studying in military-educational institutions." It is by a group of authors with advanced degrees in history and in military sciences. According to the preface, it is a "continuation of the work, *Problems of Strategy and Operational Art in Soviet Military Works*, published in 1965." The book was recommended reading in the 1972 *Calendar of a Soldier* and *Red Star*; and on November 12, 1972, this work, together with the 1965 publication, *Problems of Strategy and Operational Art*, was announced as one of six writings nominated for a Frunze Prize in 1973. This work is more than a history; it is also a vehicle in which the Soviet leadership presents a view of nonnuclear warfare.

6. Bagramyan, I. Kh., Marshal of the Soviet Union, editor, *The History of War and of Military Art* (Istoriya Voyn i Voyennovo Iskusstva), Voyenizdat, 1970, 53,000 copies, 560 pages. This work is by a group of authors of the Malinovskiy Tank Academy and the Frunze Military Academy. It is intended as a textbook for student officers of the higher military schools of the Soviet Armed Forces. The last hundred pages discuss contemporary warfare.

7. Grekov, V. A., and Kuz'min, A. T., editors, *The "Dvina" Maneuvers* (Manevry "Dvina"), Belarus Publishing House, Minsk, 1970, 35,000 copies, 400 pages. Readers should note that this work was prepared for the printers by the Department of Propaganda and Agitation of the Central Committee of the Communist Party of Belo-

russia, and the Political Department of the Belorussian Military District. It consists of a series of articles, showing the various phases of the maneuvers. The nuclear phase of the exercise is included.

8. Shablinkov, N. I., Rear Admiral, *"Okean"* (Okean), Voyenizdat, 1970, 20,000 copies, 208 pages. This is also a selection of articles concerning the maneuvers, the first of which was written by Marshal Grechko. The photographs are excellent.

9. Staritsyn, V. S., Colonel, *The Soviet Officer* (Sovetskiy Ofitser), Voyenizdat, 1970, 30,000 copies, 328 pages. The work consists of a series of articles by Soviet officers and journalists. The opening article, "True Sons of the People," is by the Minister of Defense, Marshal A. A. Grechko. This is a Soviet "public relations" effort.

10. Sekistov, V. A., Colonel, Doctor of Historical Sciences, *War and Politics* (Voyna i Politika), Voyenizdat, 1970, 22,000 copies, 496 pages. The work concerns Western Europe and the Mediterranean area. It is intended for officers and generals of the Soviet Armed Forces, and also for readers interested in the history of World War II. In the main, the subject matter is World War II and the opening of the Second Front.

11. Skvortsov, A. N., *Preparation of the Youth for the Defense of the Country* (Gotovit' Molodezh' k Zashchite Rodiny), DOSAAF Publishing House, 1970, 65,000 copies, 104 pages. This is a very basic book, showing various examples of how collective farms, factories, and the like help to train the youth for their future military service.

12. Chuyev, Yu. V., *Operational Research in Military Affairs* (Issledovaniye Operatsiy v Voyennom Dele), Voyenizdat, 1970, 11,000 copies, 256 pages. The book is intended "for a wide circle of military readers and may also be used by workers in defense industries." This technical work has an excellent bibliography.

13. Nikol'skiy, N. M., *The Scientific-Technical Revolution: The World Economy, Politics and Population* (Nauchno-Teknicheskaya Revolyutsiya: Mirovaya Ekonomika, Politika, Naseleniye), Interna-

tional Relations Publishing House, 1970, 9,000 copies, 280 pages. An overview, from the Soviet viewpoint, of the scientific revolution throughout the world. One section, pp. 151-164, deals with "the displacement in the international balances of forces under the influence of the military-technical revolution and its consequences."

14. Andrukhov, I. I., Colonel, *The Airborne Troops of NATO* (Vozdushno-Desantnyye Voyska NATO), Voyenizdat, 1970, 16,000 copies, 240 pages. The book is "intended for officers and readers interested in the armed forces of the capitalist countries." It is of interest in that it shows some of the Soviet perceptions of NATO. This work leans heavily on US sources in its discussion of NATO's airborne forces.

15. Babin, A. I., *F. Engels—Notable Military Theoretician of the Working Class* (F. Engels—Vydayushchiysya Voyennyy Teoretik Rabochevo Klassa), Voyenizdat, 1970, 21,000 copies 320 pages. "The book is to help officers, generals, and admirals in studying the military-theoretical inheritance of classical Marxism-Leninism . . . it deals with Marxist-Leninist preparation in studying military affairs." Recommended reading in the 1972 *Calendar of a Soldier.*

16. Lomov, B. F., Corresponding Member of Academy of Pedagogical Sciences, Professor, editor, *Military-Engineering Psychology* (Voyennaya Inzhenernaya Psikhologiya), Voyenizdat, 1970, 20,000 copies, 400 pages. A collective work "for a wide circle of readers—commanders, political officers, military engineers, and doctors." The authors note that "the revolution in miiltary affairs has brought into being new branches of psychology—military-engineering psychology, the relationship of men and machines in complicated systems of management." Both the 1971 *Officer's Handbook* and the 1972 *Calendar of a Soldier* list this as recommended reading.

17. Kirshin, Yu. Ya., *On the Scientific Organization of Military Labor* (O Nauchnoy Organizatsii Voinskovo Truda), Voyenizdat, 1970, 24,000 copies, 120 pages. The authors note that "methods of industry, which were used freely in conditions of nuclear rocket war, have undergone basic changes." The work is intended for commanders, political workers, engineers, and technical workers, as well

as for a wide circle of military readers. It is listed as recommended reading in the "Soldier's Bookshelf."

18. Babadzhanyan, A. Kh., Marshal of Armored Troops, editor, *Tanks and Tank Troops* (Tank i Tankovyye Voyska), Voyenizdat, 1970, 9,000 copies, 336 pages. The first part of the work concerns the creation of armored equipment and the significance of the appearance of nuclear weapons. The second part deals with the question of the military use of tanks in contemporary warfare. Of particular interest is the discussion of nuclear explosions and tanks. Listed in *Calendar of a Soldier*, 1972.

1971

The 24th Party Congress met in the early Spring of 1971, and was marked by the appearance of a series of major books. These writings can be compared with the writings that were published during the Khrushchev era, as well as during the 23rd Party Congress in 1966. Such comparisons should greatly assist the analyst in determining what shifts in doctrine and strategy, if any, have taken place.

1. Grechko, A. A., Marshal of the Soviet Union, Minister of Defense, *On Guard Over the Peace and the Building of Communism* (Na Strazhe Mira i Stroitel'stva Kommunizma), Voyenizdat, 1971, 200,000 copies, 112 pages. This is the most authoritative single work on Soviet military doctrine and strategy since the publication in 1962 of Marshal Malinovskiy's famed work, *Vigilantly Stand Guard Over the Peace*. The book is recommended reading in *Calendar of a Soldier*, 1972. It has been translated into English.

2. Kozlov, S. N. General Major (Reserve), Candidate of Military Sciences, editor, *The Officer's Handbook* (Spravochnik Ofitsera), Voyenizdat, 1971, 83,000 copies, 400 pages. Among the many well-known contributors to this work were General Major Ye. F. Sulimov, Doctor of Philosophical Sciences; Colonel V. V. Mochalov, Candidate of Military Sciences; and Colonel S. A. Tyushkevich, Doctor of Philosophical Sciences: The work is intended for officers of all ser-

vices in the Soviet Armed Forces, and primarily for young officers. A fairly comprehensive overview of the Soviet Armed Forces is given, including basic concepts of military doctrine, strategy, and art. The bibliography at the end of each chapter is of particular interest for those who wish to study further in the area discussed. This is the 15th publication of the "Officer's Library" series, and is listed as recommended reading in the 1972 *Calendar of a Soldier*. It has been translated into English.

3. Strokov, A. A., General Major, Professor, *V. I. Lenin on War and Military Art* (V. I. Lenin o Voyne i Voyennom Iskusstve), Nauka Publishing House, 1971, 10,000 copies, 184 pages. This interesting Soviet paperback, issued by the Academy of Sciences Publishing House, notes inside the front cover that Strokov is a General Major and a Professor. It is very significant book, dealing with subjects from military doctrine to the idea of "little wars."

4. Azovtsev, N. N., Colonel, Doctor of Historical Science, *V. I. Lenin and Soviet Military Science* (V. I. Lenin i Sovetskaya Voyennaya Nauka), Nauka Publishing House, 1971, 4,600 copies, 360 pages. This is another military work published by the Academy of Sciences Publishing House, and compares with Colonel Strokov's work, listed above, in interest. For some reason, the publishers did not list the author's military rank, and the casual reader might not be aware of the fact that he is an expert on military history at the Institute of Military History of the Ministry of Defense. He discusses the laws of war as being one of the most important tasks of Soviet military science, and notes that "only in recent years has a group of books been published in which are reflected the various sides of this big problem, having great theoretical and practical significance." Pp. 276-344 provide excellent statements of Soviet doctrine, strategy, military science, and views concerning the use of nuclear weapons.

5. Yakubovskiy, I. I., Marshal of the Soviet Union, Commander in Chief of the Warsaw Pact Forces, *Fighting Cooperation* (Boyevoye Sodruzhestvo), Voyenizdat, 1971, 200,000 copies, 104 pages. Like Marshal Grechko's work, *On Guard Over the Peace and the Building of Communism*, Yakubovskiy's pamphlet explains the de-

cisions of the 24th Party Congress. Primarily, he discusses the formation of the Warsaw Pact Forces. Recommended in the 1972 *Calendar of a Soldier*.

6. Yepishev, A. A., General of the Army, Chief of the Main Political Administration of the Soviet Army and Navy, *Communists of the Army and Navy* (Kommunisty Armii i Flota), Voyenizdat, 200,000 copies, 96 pages. Like the works of Grechko and Yakubovskiy, Yepishev also has the task of explaining the decisions of the 24th Party Congress. He discusses "the raising of military preparedness and the discipline of the troops." This work also is on the shelves of the 1972 *Calendar of a Soldier*.

7. Grudinin, I. A., Colonel, Doctor of Philosophical Sciences, *Dialetics and Contemporary Military Affairs* (Dialektika i Sovremennoye Voyennoye Delo), Voyenizdat, 1971, 28,000 copies, 320 pages. Grudinin died in 1970, shortly before his book appeared. Over the past decade, he had been one of the best known of the Soviet military theorists, writing generally on the application of the dialectic to military doctrine and strategy. This work touches on the sensitive areas of local wars, surprise attack, civil defense, and the Strategic Rocket Troops. Another 1972 *Calendar of a Soldier* recommendation.

8. Bagramyan, I. Kh., Marshal of the Soviet Union, editor, *Military History* (Voyennaya Istoriya), Voyenizdat, 1971, 60,000 copies, 352 pages. Faculty members from the Malinovskiy Tank Academy, the Frunze Military Academy, and the Lenin Military-Political Academy contributed to this work. In general, the book is a basic military history textbook. The last section discusses contemporary warfare.

9. Bartenev, S. A., Colonel, Candidate of Economic Sciences, *Economics: The Rear and the Front of Contemporary War* (Ekonomika: Tyl i Front Sovremennoy Voyny), Voyenizdat, 1971, 10,000 copies, 192 pages. Soviet perceptions of the role of economics in the industrial power of the United States, and the impact of the United States economy during World War II are the main themes of this book. The author notes that "with the appearance of the nuclear-rocket weapon, the preparation of the economics of the rear for the

demands of war has taken on new aspects." Maintaining an economy in time of war is now greatly complicated by the fact that the ICBM can deliver a thermonuclear weapon to any spot on the globe.

10. Zheltov, A. S., General Colonel, editor, *The Soldier and War* (Soldat i Voyna), Voyenizdat, 1971, 43,000 copies, 320 pages. This book is a collective work by writers at the Lenin Military-Political Academy. The authors have advanced degrees in military sciences, philosophical sciences, psychology, and history. "Moral-political problems and the psychological preparation of the Soviet soldier" take up the greater part of the text. Of special note are the methods of indoctrination used in each of the five services (pp. 266-316). A 1972 *Calendar of a Soldier* recommendation.

11. Milovidov, A. S., Colonel, Doctor of Philosophical Sciences, Professor, *Communist Morality and Military Duty* (Kommunistiche-skaya Moral i Voinskiy Dolg), Voyenizdat, 1971, 30,000 copies, 184 pages. A work written for commanders, political workers, propagandists, agitators, and Party and Komsomol activists. It is interesting to read this publication in light of the current situation existing in the US armed forces. Recommended in the 1972 *Calendar of a Soldier.*

12. Borisov, B. A., *Our Mighty Army* (Armiya Nasha Moguchaya), Voyenizdat, 1971, 30,000 copies, 128 pages. Intended for young soldiers and for youth preparing for service in the Soviet Armed Forces, the work reflects the basic Soviet concepts of military doctrine and strategy.

13. Ponomaryev, A. N., General Colonel-Engineer, Doctor of Technical Sciences, *Aviation at the Threshold of the Cosmos* (Aviatsiya Na Poroge v Kosmos), Voyenizdat, 1971, 11,700 copies 320 pages. A book for pilots, engineers, and members of technical staffs. Much of the material is from the foreign press. Because of traditional Russian secrecy, examples of US and other non-Soviet aircraft are given. The work reflects some Soviet concepts, but contains little of a substantive nature.

14. Peresada, S. A., Lieutenant Colonel-Engineer, Candidate of Technical Sciences, Filippov, A. I., Demidov, L. I., *The Struggle with*

Low-Flying Means of Air Attack (Bor'ba s Nizkoletyashchimi Sredst-
vami Vozdushnovo Napadeniya), Voyenizdat, 1971, 10,000 copies, 176 pages. Much of the material is taken from "the foreign
press"—meaning the US and Western Europe. The book suggests the
great Soviet interest in Western aviation tactics.

15. Arkhangel'skiy A. M., *Bacteriological Weapons and Defense
Against Them* (Bakteriologicheskoye Oruzhiye i Zashchita ot Nevo),
Voyenizdat, 1971, 100,000 copies, 208 pages. This is a "popular
science library" book, intended for a wide circle of readers. It is of
interest to note the considerable number of copies printed, and the
views of the author on the possibility of the use of weapons of this
type.

16. Naumenko, I. A., Pavlov, M. P., Ivanov, A. I., *The Nuclear
Rocket Weapon and Its Destructive Action* (Raketno-Yadernoye
Oruzhiye i Yevo Porazhayushcheye Deystviye), Voyenizdat, 1971,
60,000 copies, 224 pages. Like the book on bacteriological weapons,
this is another "popular science library" book. A considerable portion of the work is based on material from the US press. The reader
is able to gain some appreciation of the popular view in the Soviet
Union of the nuclear-rocket weapon and of possible defenses against
it.

17. Ivanov, D. A., Savel'yev, V. P., Shemanskiy, P. V., *The Basis
of Directing Troops* (Osnovy Upravleniya Voyskami), Voyenizdat,
1971, 13,000 copies, 384 pages. This work is intended "for officers
and generals of the armed forces." The first portion of the book concerns the development of troop leadership with respect to the appearance of the nuclear weapon. There is some discussion of "the postwar
revolution in military affairs and its influence on directing troops."
Demands of leadership in contemporary conditions are summed up on
pp. 67-78.

18. Malikov, V. G., Komisarik, S. F., Korotkov, A. N., *Ground-
Handling Equipment of Rockets* (Nazemnoye Oborudovaniye Rakety), Voyenizdat, 1971, 10,000 copies, 304 pages. "For commanders
and engineer-technical troops of rocket units," and also for officers
of the Soviet Army, students of military academies, and students of

special faculties of higher military schools," this work discusses ground-handling equipment for rockets of various designations, from ICBMs to tactical nuclear rockets.

1972

Soviet military-theoretical writings published in the year of the Moscow Summit Meeting were of special interest, although they were relatively few in number. Negotiators in SALT, MBFR, and the European Security Conference should find the first four books listed below of particular value.

1. Savkin, V. Ye., Colonel, Candidate of Military Sciences, *The Basic Principles of Operational Art and Tactics* (Osnovnyye Printsipy Operativnovo Iskusstva i Taktiki), Voyenizdat, 1972, 13,000 copies, 376 pages. This work is "intended for officers and generals of the Soviet Army," and is recommended for "discussion." Some of the concepts given are "most complicated, and are located at the junction of military art and philosophy." The views of the author on the tactical use of nuclear weapons, the element of surprise, and other aspects of warfare are among the most challenging yet presented in the Soviet open press. This is a major work.

2. Rotmistrov, P. A., Chief Marshal of Armored Forces, Doctor of Military Sciences, Professor, *Time and the Tank* (Vremya i Tanki), Voyenizdat, 1972, 30,000 copies, 336 pages. Although the greater part of this work deals with history prior to and during World War II, the last few pages make the work of particular significance. Very briefly and concisely, Rotmistrov discusses the postwar build-up of the Soviet Armed Forces, with emphasis on the role of the tank in conditions of nuclear-rocket war. This is of particular interest to those concerned with the Soviet view of the tactical use of nuclear weapons.

3. Yefremov, A. Ye., Doctor of Historical Sciences, *Europe and the Nuclear Weapon* (Yevropa i Yadernoye Oruzhiye), International Relations Publishing House, Moscow, 1972, 8,500 copies, 392 pages. In the frontispiece, Dr. V. M. Kulish is listed as the "reviewer." Dr.

Kulish, a former colonel and military strategist on the General Staff, was on the staff of the Institute of World Economy and International Relations (IMEMO), and is a recognized Soviet authority on United States foreign policy and defense. This book represents a dialogue of sorts in the Soviet preparation for SALT II and the European Security Conference. It reflects Soviet perceptions and misconceptions of NATO and its tactical nuclear weapons.

4. Popov, V. I., Professor, editor, *Soviet Foreign Policy and European Security* (Sovetskaya Vneshnyaya Politika i Yevropeyskaya Bezopasnost'), International Relations Publishing House, Moscow, 1972, 15,000 copies, 254 pages. This work is introduced by A. P. Shitikov, a representative of the Soviet Committee for European Security. One chapter is by Anat. A. Gromyko, son of the Soviet Foreign Minister and a former staff member of the Institute of the USA. This work provides insights into Soviet concepts of their doctrine and strategy.

5. Korobeynikov, M. P., Colonel, Doctor of Psychological Sciences, *Contemporary Battle and Problems of Psychology* (Sovremennyy Boy i Problemy Psikhologii), Voyenizdat, 1972, 38,000 copies, 240 pages. The book examines the psychological preparation of troops, and the problem of achieving success in conditions of nuclear-rocket warfare. It is intended for a wide circle of readers.

6. Sorokin, Yu., editor, *Bridgehead Beyond the Clouds* (Platsdarm za Oblakami), Young Guards Publishing House, 1972, 100,000 copies, 192 pages. This book is intended to interest Soviet youth in the Airborne Forces. The frontispiece carries a statement by one of the early cosmonauts, G. S. Titov. The work consist of a series of articles, with many photographs. It is a smooth public relations publication.

7. Dzyza, A. M., General Major, editor, *Textbook for the Sergeants of the Troops of PVO* (Posobiye Serzhanty Voysk PVO), Voyenizdat, 1972, 45,000 copies, 200 pages. Specific examples of Soviet military organization and training are given in this book. Concepts of doctrine, strategy, and types of weapon systems are reflected in the examples of training that are shown.

8. Durov, V. R., *The Combat Use and the Combat Effectiveness of Fighter-Interceptors* (Boyevoye Primeneniye i Boyevaya Effektivnost' Istrebiteley-Perekhvatchikov), Voyenizdat, 1972, 8,000 copies, 280 pages. This book is intended for PVO pilots, students, and workers in the aviation industry. It is very technical, and of interest in that it provides Soviet insights into the effectiveness of interceptor aircraft.

9. Plyaskin, V. Ya., General Lieutenant, Professor, Candidate of Military Sciences; Lysukhin, I. F., Colonel, Docent, Candidate of Military Sciences; Ruvinskiy, V. A., Colonel, Docent, Candidate of Technical Services, *Engineering Support of Combined Arms Battle* (Inzhenernoye Obespecheniye Obshchevoyskovovo Boya), Voyenizdat, 1972, 368 pages. Intended for Ground Forces officers and students attending military schools, this book provides examples of Ground Forces tactics and types of engineering equipment that might be used in support. Some examples are given from the "foreign press," but Soviet equipment is also included.

10. Karpenko, P. I., Colonel, Candidate of Historical Sciences, editor, *Party-Political Work in the Soviet Armed Forces* (Partiyno-Politicheskaya Rabota v Sovetskikh Vooruzhennykh Silakh), 1972, 50,000 copies, 288 pages. This is a textbook for military students attending civilian institutions. Of particular interest are the statements on the role of the Party in the formulation of Soviet military doctrine.

11. Badmayev, B. Ts., Lieutenant Colonel, Candidate of Psychological Sciences, *An Important Factor in Combat Readiness* (Vazhnyy Faktor Boyegotovnosti), 25,000 copies, 216 pages. Examples "from the experience of the moral-political and psychological preparation of the troops" are presented in this book. It is intended for commanders, political workers, engineers, technicians, and active Party units and on ships. The opening article is by General of the Army A. A. Yepishev, Head of the Main Political Administration.

12. Abchuk, V. A., Yemel'yanov, L. A., Suzdal', V. G., *Introduction to the Theory of the Working Out of Decisions* (Vvedeniye v Teoriyu Vyrabotki Resheniy), Voyenizdat, 1972, 8,000 copies, 344

pages. This work is intended for officers, generals, admirals of the Navy, scientific workers, students of military schools and institutions. It discusses game theory, cybernetics, and mathematical modeling, and the possible application of these theories to wartime decision-making. The authors provide a comparison of the state of Soviet war-gaming with that in the United States.

13. *Comrade* (Tovarishch), The Young Guard Publishing House, 1972, 200,000 copies, 400 pages. The Soviet *Pioneer Handbook* is very similar in size and in content to the *Boy Scout Handbook* in the United States. Even to one who cannot read Russian, however, the differences are obvious and important. Any student of Soviet military doctrine and strategy should examine this work in order to see how Soviet military thought is presented in the indoctrination of the youth of the USSR.

14. Druzhinin, V. V. and Kontorov, D. S., *Idea, Algorithm, Decision* (Ideya, Algoritm, Resheniye), Voyenizdat, 1972, 30,000 copies, 328 pages. This book is one of the "Officer's Library" series. It deals with the possible utilization of computers throughout the Soviet Armed Forces, and how such computers might assist the military commander in making decisions on the battlefield. The book is for a wide circle of readers—commanders, operators, and engineers —wishing to understand and to deepen their knowledge about the automation of data as an aid to decisionmaking.

15. Milovidov, A. S., General Major, Doctor of Philosophical Sciences, Professor, and Kozlov, V. G., Colonel, Candidate of Philosophical Sciences, Docent, *The Philosophical Heritage of V. I. Lenin and Problems of Contemporary War* (Filosofskoye Naslediye V. I. Lenin i Problemy Sovremennoy Voyny), Voyenizdat, 1972, 27,000 copies, 392 pages. A most significant work which restates Soviet military-political views on the nature of war, expressed during the time of the 1972 Moscow Summit Meeting. Contributing authors include V. M. Bondarenko and Ye. I. Rybkin, considered at one time as the Soviet "Red Hawks." The work is "for officers and generals and others studying the military-theoretical heritage of V. I. Lenin." The chapter on civil defense is of particular interest and should give readers cause for reflection.

1973

Following the 1972 Moscow Summit Meeting, at which time the SALT I agreements were signed, Western analysts were most interested in determining whether or not the "detente" might have any impact upon Soviet military thought.

The analyst of Soviet military thought will find the third edition of the *Bolshaya Encyclopedia* of great value. Publication of this edition began in 1970, and by mid-1974 was approximately half-completed. The discussion of military doctrine and strategy in this encyclopedia, as well as basic data given on the Soviet Armed Forces, can be compared with that appearing in various publications over the past decade.

The following books, published in 1973, permit the Western reader to judge for himself whether the basic concepts of the Soviet Armed Forces were changed as a result of the detente.

1. Lomov, N. A., General Colonel, Professor, *Scientific-Technical Progress and the Revolution in Military Affairs* (Nauchno-Tekni-cheskiy Progress i Revolyutsiya v Voyennom Dele), Voyenizdat, 1973, 40,000 copies, 280 pages. This work is probably the most significant publication concerning Soviet military doctrine and strategy since *Military Strategy* appeared in 1968. It is a collective work, with General Lomov as the editor, and also the author of the Introduction and Conclusion. Lomov, a former instructor on Soviet military doctrine at the General Staff Academy, is a consultant to the Institute of the USA. Among the other contributors to the work are both Colonels Bondarenko and Rybkin of the Lenin Military-Political Academy, as well as noted spokesmen of the General Staff Academy. According to *Red Star*, this book will be the last of the "Officer's Library" series.

2. Baranov, B. I., General Lieutenant, *Textbook for Teaching the Young Soldier* (Posobiye Po Obucheniyu Melodykh Soldat), Voyenizdat, 1973. Most Soviet books list the number of copies published. Apparently, the number of textbooks published for the "young soldier" is a military secret, and hence is not given. The textbook

consists of 308 pages. This work "may be used by the young soldier for self-preparation." Given in the book are practical instructions and advice for the draftee on markmanship, scouting, drill, physical training, and the like. This is a very practical work. It is interesting to compare with writings on military doctrine and strategy, intended for "officers and generals."

3. Sulimov, Ye. F., General Major, Doctor of Philosophical Sciences and Shelyag, V. V., Rear Admiral, Doctor of Philosophical Sciences, *Problems of the Scientific Leadership of the Soviet Armed Forces* (Voprosy Nauchnovo Rukovodstva v Sovetskikh Vooruzhennykh Silakh), Voyenizdat, 1973, 28,000 copies, 268 pages. In this book, the authors seek to bring together the "scientific" methods of Marxism-Leninism and modern computer technology. General Major Sulimov is one of the most articulate Soviet military-political spokesmen, and a former Frunze prize winner. For those who "mirror-image" the Soviet Union, this book may be most revealing.

4. Lepeshkin, A. I., Professor, Colonel, Justice, *The Fundamentals of Soviet Military Legislation* (Osnovy Sovetskovo Voyennovo Zakonodatel'stva), Voyenizdat, 1973, 100,000 copies, 272 pages. This is a "textbook for students of higher military-political schools." It is also recommended for "commanders, political-workers, engineers, Party and Komsomol activists in the Army and Navy." It is interesting to read this book in conjunction with a book explaining the legal system of the armed forces of the United States. The differences will quickly become apparent.

5. Radziyevskiy, A. I., General of the Army, Professor, *The Academy Named for M. V. Frunze* (Akademiya Imeni M. V. Frunze), Voyenizdat, 1973, 22,000 copies, 280 pages. The Frunze Military Academy ranks second only to the General Staff Academy in the Soviet military education system. In addition to these two academies, there are 15 other academies in the Soviet military structure. These institutions roughly compare to the war colleges in the United States. The commandants of the academies rate four stars, the same as military district commanders. This book provides general information on this famed institute. Visitors to Moscow should view at least

the outside of this academy, which is located on Devich'yevo Proyezd, within walking distance of the United States Embassy.

6. Danchenko, A. M., Colonel, Candidate of Pedagogical Sciences and Vydrin, I. F., Colonel, Candidate of Pedagogical Sciences, *Military Pedagogics* (Voyennaya Pedagogika), Voyenizdat, 1973, 150,000 copies, 368 pages. This is a textbook for the higher military-political schools, which provides four-year courses for political officers. These officers are the instructors in the Soviet Armed Forces, except for those providing instruction of a specific technical nature. The book is most useful in indicating the teaching methods used in the Soviet Armed Forces, as well as providing some idea of the content of the teaching.

7. Shelyag, V. V., Rear Admiral, Doctor of Philosophical Sciences, *Problems of the Psychology of the Military Collective* (Problemy Psikhologii Voinskovo Kollektiva), Voyenizdat, 1973, 55,000 copies, 302 pages. The "moral-political and psychological preparation" of military personnel is the theme of this book. One chapter is given to a discussion of military psychological problems in groups, collectives, and among the leadership in foreign armies. This work is a worthwhile study for the analyst concerned with the importance of ideology in the Soviet Armed Forces.

8. Smukul, A. O., and Fedurin, A. S., *The Tyl (Rear Services) of the Navy* (Tyl Voyenno-Morskikh Sil), 4,000 copies, 268 pages, Voyenizdat, 1973. This work is intended for specialists in naval support and for students in naval and ship-construction schools. Most of the examples given are from the foreign press. Many of the photographs of ships and naval facilities are of the United States Navy. This is a standard feature of Soviet books dealing with equipment. The leadership wants the members of the Soviet Armed Forces to understand modern equipment, but their security practices are such that very little of their own military hardware can be displayed in the Soviet press. Hence, examples from the Western press are used.

9. Peresada, S. A., *Ground-to-Air Rocket Complexes* (Zenitnyye Raketnyye Kompleksy), Voyenizdat, 1973, 12,000 copies, 272 pages. Any foreign tourist flying into the Soviet Union may see the numerous surface-to-air missile sites that surround each large Soviet city. How-

ever, except for carefully censored photographs that appear from time to time in the Soviet press, these installations are "secret." Hence, any Soviet book showing details of surface-to-air missiles and the nature of the construction site must use materials from the foreign press. This post-SALT I book is of interest in that it indicates high Soviet attention to antiair missile sites, at a time when the United States has dropped the idea of providing continental defense against manned aircraft.

10. Volovich, V. K. and Kuznetsov, N. I., *People's Control in the Armed Forces of the USSR* (Narodnyy Kontrol' v Vooruzhennykh Silakh SSSR), Voyenizdat, 28,000 copies, 206 pages. Soviet theoretical literature stresses the "people's" control of the Soviet Armed Forces. This book is for the "activists in people's control, and also for commanders and party-political workers." According to the fly-leaf, "in the book are examined basic questions of the activities of the organs of people's control in the Soviet Armed Forces." Books such as this provide insights into the Party-military system of the Soviet Union.

11. Gorniy, A. G., General Colonel, Justice, *The Fundamentals of Legal Knowledge* (Osnovy Pravovykh Znaniy), Voyenizdat, 1973, 43,000 copies, 424 pages. Great attention is paid in the United States to Soviet weapon systems. Very little is known about the actual composition and workings of the Soviet Armed Forces as a whole. This book provides details of Soviet military life—hours of work, pensions, military courts, and so forth—that are almost unknown to most analysts in the United States unless they read Russian. This textbook is written for use in the two-year courses on "legal knowledge" that are given at each Soviet garrison by the "Military Knowledge Societies."

12. Yepishev, A. A., General of the Army, *The Powerful Weapon of the Party* (Mogucheye Oruzhiye Partii), Voyenizdat, 1973, 50,000 copies, 320 pages. General Yepishev is head of the Main Political Administration of the Soviet Army and Navy, and ranks Number Four in the Soviet military hierarchy. His organization has the rights of a department under the Central Committee. General Yepishev, with his direct tie to the Party structure, serves as the Party's watch-

dog over the Soviet Armed Forces. This book discusses Party organization and ideological work among the Soviet military.

13. Malopurin, I. I., Colonel-Engineer, Docent, Candidate of Psychological Sciences, *The Psychological Basis of Teaching Tank Troops* (Psikhologichesekiye Osnovy Obucheniya Tankistov), Voyenizdat, 1973, 14,000 copies, 197 pages. The book attempts to show how, through careful psychological training, tank troops can gain complete confidence in their equipment and be capable of waging battle under varying conditions. Analysts interested in the methods of training Soviet soldiers should find this work of value.

1974

In 1974, Soviet spokesmen were highly cautious. Care had to be taken to ensure that the population recognized the need to continue sacrifices in support of the defense effort. At the same time, the "capitalist" powers must not be alarmed by the military press to the point where arms negotiations would seem futile. A careful reading of Soviet military and political-military publications was necessary to follow the continuity of Soviet military thought. The following books warrant study:

1. Grechko, A. A., Marshal of the Soviet Union, Minister of Defense, Member of Politburo, *The Armed Forces of the Soviet State* (Vooruzhennyye Sily Sovetskovo Gosudarstva), Voyenizdat, 1974, 50,000 copies, 406 pages. This book was, in all probability, the most important work on Soviet military affairs for 1974. The Minister of Defense discusses all apects of the Soviet Armed Forces—military doctrine and strategy, the revolution in military affairs, tactical nuclear war, types of war, superiority, preventing strikes, civil defense, and so forth. Grechko's work should be required reading for all analysts. It was not submitted to the publisher until after the 1973 October War in the Middle East.

2. Titov, M. N., *Civil Defense* (Grazhdanskaya Oborona), Higher School Publishing House, 600,000 copies, 215 pages, 1974. Essentially a textbook on civil defense for students in "middle schools,"

which roughly correspond to high schools in the United States, this book covers civil defense measures for personnel in industry, agriculture, and other occupations. It is a comprehensive work. It is in accordance with the basic tenet of Soviet military doctrine that "the armed forces, the nation, and the entire population must be prepared for the eventuality of a nuclear-rocket war."

3. Yepishev, A. A., General of the Army, *The Ideological Struggle on Military Problems* (Ideologicheskaya Bor'ba Po Voyennym Voprosam), Voyenizdat, 1974, 50,000 copies, 120 pages. One characteristic of the "detente," as considered by the Soviet Union, is the intensification of the ideological struggle. In this book, General Yepishev, Chief of the Main Political Administration of the Soviet Army and Navy, follows the dictates of the Central Committee of the Communist Party in explaining the ideological content of "detente." These views, an integral part of the Soviet concept of relations with the outside world, are seldom recognized in the West.

4. Kondratyuk, K. A., editor, *People and the Cause of Civil Defense* (Lyudi i Dela Grazhdanskoy Oborony), Voyenizdat, 1974, 30,000 copies, 152 pages. This book consists of a series of articles on civil defense. The opening article, by General Colonel A. Altunin, Deputy Minister of Defense and Chief of Civil Defense, provides some data about contemporary civil defense in the Soviet Union. Included also is a fairly interesting article about the newly formed civil defense school for officers, and another on the establishment of a civil defense unit at a factory. The remainder of the articles generally concern civil defense during World War II.

5. Sredin, G. V. General Colonel, editor, *On Guard Over the Motherland* (Na Strazhye Rodiny), Voyenizdat, 1974, 335 pages. This work is a textbook for use in political studies. Two major themes are discussed: (1) the Armed Forces of the USSR on guard over the gains of the October Revolution, and (2) the need for constant readiness for the armed defense of the Motherland—the Union of Soviet Socialist Republics. A very good summary of the development of the Soviet Armed Forces and their role today is provided in the first section. Soviet perceptions of the armed forces of "capitalist" nations are given in the second part of the book. Of particular interest is the

concept of combat readiness, as presented in a course in political studies.

6. Bezuglov, I. G., *Komsomol Work in the Soviet Army and Navy* (Komsomol'skaya Rabota v Sovetskoy Armii i Flotye), Voyenizdat, 1974, 60,000 copies, 264 pages. Relatively few Westerners appreciate or understand the role of the Komsomols in the Soviet Union, and particularly in the Soviet Armed Forces. Over 90 percent of Soviet officers either are Komsomol or Communist Party members. This book is used as a textbook. It is designed for study by students attending evening classes in political schools, and in Komsomol activities of military subunits and units on ships.

7. Beskurnikov, A., composing editor, *Strike and Defend* (Udar i Zashchita), Young Guards Publishing House, 1974, 100,000 copies, 208 pages. Each service and each branch of a service of the Soviet Armed Forces presents a series of books for teenage Soviet youth. This particular book glorifies the Tank Troops. The opening article is by Marshal of Tank Troops A. Kh. Babadzhanyan. Tank training in general is covered in other articles.

8. Lavrik, M. S., editor, *Ordered to Protect!* (Prikazano Zastupit'!), Young Guards Publishing House, 1974, 100,000 copies, 240 pages. Very little is known in the United States about the internal troops of the MVD (Ministry of Internal Affairs) in the Soviet Union. Such troops by Soviet law are an integral part of the Soviet Armed Forces, but are not subordinate to the Ministry of Defense. This book consists of a series of articles about the MVD troops.

9. Latukhin, A. N., *Antitank Weapons* (Protivotankovoye Vooruzheniye), Voyenizdat, 1974, 15,500 copies, 270 pages. Tanks and antitank weapons receive great attention in Soviet military publications. This particular work was prepared "for a wide circle of readers interested in contemporary weapons and military equipment." As is customary in Soviet publications dealing with military technology, most of the examples and photographs shown are from the "foreign press." Despite these examples, the book does indicate some current Soviet views on antitank warfare.

10. Morozov, N. I., *Ballistic Rockets of Strategic Designation* (Ballisticheskiye Rakety Strategicheskovo Naznacheniya), Voyenizdat, 1974, 10,000 copies, 208 pages. In the main, the examples and technical data in this work are taken from the "foreign press." The book is "intended for a wide circle of readers" interested in military rocket technology. Tables list details of rockets possessed by Western nations; but, as is customary, nothing is given on Soviet weapons. Certain provisions of the SALT I agreements are given in the appendix. Omitted, however, is that portion of the agreements which list numbers of weapons permitted to the Soviet Union.

11. Gatsolayev, V. A., *Air Defense of Subunits in Battle* (Zenitnyye Podrazdeleniya v Boyu), Voyenizdat, 1974, 11,000 copies, 144 pages. As a result of the study of combat actions in Southeast Asia and the Middle East, Soviet military theoreticians are carefully reviewing air defense weapons and techniques for their Ground Forces. This book opens with an analysis, including photographs, of aircraft and armaments, especially helicopters, of Western nations. The second half of the book shows typical methods of attack used by Western pilots, and what methods of defense might be used by troops on the ground against such attacks.

5

English Translations of Soviet Military Books

The following books, listed in the preceding bibliography, have already been translated into English:

1. Sokolovskiy, V. D., Marshal of the Soviet Union, editor, *Military Strategy*, 3rd edition (1968). Translation, analysis, and commentary by Harriet Fast Scott. Crane, Russak and Company, publishers, New York, 1975. This translation identifies all changes made among the first, second, and third editions, and also includes those portions that were dropped between the publication of the earlier and the third editions.

2. Malinovskiy, R. Ya., Marshal of the Soviet Union, *Vigilantly Stand Guard Over the Peace* (1962). Translation not identified.

3. Kuusinen, O. V., editor, *The Fundamentals of Marxism-Leninism* (1962). This work was translated into English and published by Foreign Languages Publishing House, Moscow, in 1963. Since the book made frequent references to Khrushchev, publication ceased after 1964.

4. Reznichenko, V. G., General Major, *Tactics* (1966). Translated by the Foreign Technological Division, Wright-Patterson AFB, Ohio.

5. Astashenkov, P. T., Colonel, *Soviet Rocket Troops* (1967). Translated by JPRS.

6. Modrzhinskaya, Ye. D., *et al.*, *Problems of War and Peace* (1967). Translated by the Foreign Technological Division, Wright-Patterson AFB, Ohio. In 1972, Progress Publishers, Moscow, issued an updated version of this book in English.

7. Tyushkevich, S. A., Colonel, *Marxism-Leninism on War and the Army* (1968). An English edition of this work was issued by Progress Publishers, Moscow, in 1972.

8. Krasovskiy, S. A., editor, *Aviation and Cosmonautics* (1967). English translation not identified.

9. Khmel', A. Ye., General Lieutenant, *Party-Political Work in the Soviet Armed Forces* (1968). A somewhat abridged edition of this work was translated into English in 1972 by Progress Publishers, Moscow, entitled *Education of a Soviet Soldier: Party-Political Work in the Soviet Armed Forces.*

10. Zheltov, A. S., General Colonel, *Methodological Problems of Military Theory and Practice* (1968). Translated by the Foreign Technological Division, Wright-Patterson AFB, Ohio.

11. Lotostkiy, V. K., *Army of the Soviets* (1969). Translated into English in 1971 by Progress Publishers, Moscow, with the title *The Soviet Army.*

12. Sidorenko, A. A., Colonel, *The Offensive* (1970). Translated and published under the auspices of the United States Air Force by the US Government Printing Office, Washington, D.C. 20402. (Price $1.80, Stock No. 0870-00329.)

13. Grechko, A. A., Marshal of the Soviet Union, *On Guard Over the Peace and the Building of Communism* (1971). Translated by JPRS.

14. Kozlov, S. N., General Major, *The Officer's Handbook* (1971). Translated by the Foreign Technological Division, Wright-Patterson AFB, Ohio.

15. Savkin, V. Ye., Colonel, *Basic Principles of Operational Art and Tactics* (1972). Translated and published under the auspices of the United States Air Force, by the US Government Printing Office, Washington, D.C. 2402. (Price $2.30, Stock No. 0807-00342.)

16. Yefremov, A. Ye., *Europe and the Nuclear Weapon* (1972). Translated by JPRS.

17. Druzhinin, V. V., *Idea, Algorithm, Decision* (1972). Translated by the Foreign Technological Division, Wright-Patterson AFB, Ohio.

18. Milovidov, A. S., General Major, *et al.*, *The Philosophical Heritage of V. I. Lenin and Problems of Contemporary War* (1972). Translated and published under the auspices of the United States Air Force by the US Government Printing Office, Washington, D.C. 20402. (Price $2.35, Stock No. 0870-00343.)

19. Lomov, N. A., General Colonel, *Scientific-Technical Progress and the Revolution in Military Affairs* (1973). Translated and published under the auspices of the United States Air Force by the US Government Printing Office, Washington, D.C. 20402. (Price $2.35, Stock No. 0870-00340.)

Books numbered 2, 4, 5, 6, 8, 10, 13, 14, 16, and 17 may be ordered from:

NTIS
5285 Port Royal Road
Springfield, Virginia 22161

Books numbered 3, 7, 9, and 11 may be ordered from:

Victor Kamkin, Inc.
12224 Parklawn Drive
Rockville, Maryland 20852

National Strategy Information Center, Inc.

STRATEGY PAPERS

Edited by Frank N. Trager and William Henderson
With the assistance of Dorothy E. Nicolosi

Soviet Sources of Military Doctrine and Strategy by William F. Scott. July 1975

Detente: Promises and Pitfalls by Gerald L. Steibel, March 1975

Oil, Politics, and Sea Power: The Indian Ocean Vortex by Ian W. A. C. Adie, December 1974

The Soviet Presence in Latin America by James D. Theberge, June 1974

The Horn of Africa by J. Bowyer Bell, Jr., December 1973

Research and Development and the Prospects for International Security by Frederick Seitz and Rodney W. Nichols, December 1973

Raw Material Supply in a Multipolar World by Yuan-li Wu. October 1973

The People's Liberation Army: Communist China's Armed Forces by Angus M. Fraser, August 1973

Nuclear Weapons and the Atlantic Alliance by Wynfred Joshua, May 1973

How to Think About Arms Control and Disarmament by James E. Dougherty, May 1973

The Military Indoctrination of Soviet Youth by Leon Goure, January 1973

The Asian Alliance: Japan and United States Policy by Franz Michael and Gaston J. Sigur, October 1972

Iran, The Arabian Peninsula, and the Indian Ocean by R. M. Burrel and Alvin J. Cottrell, September 1972 (Out of print)

Soviet Naval Power: Challenge for the 1970s by Norman Polmar, April 1972. Revised edition, September 1974

How Can We Negotiate with the Communists? by Gerald L. Steibel, March 1972

Soviet Political Warfare Techniques, Espionage and Propaganda in the 1970s by Lyman B. Kirkpatrick, Jr., and Howland H. Sargeant, January 1972

The Soviet Presence in the Eastern Mediterranean by Lawrence L. Whetten, September 1971

*The Military Unbalance
Is the U.S. Becoming a Second-Class Power?* June 1971

The Future of South Vietnam by Brigadier F. P. Serong, February 1971 (Out of print)

Strategy and National Interests: Reflections for the Future by Bernard Brodie, January 1971 (Out of print)

The Mekong River: A Challenge in Peaceful Development for Southeast Asia by Eugene R. Black, December 1970 (Out of print)

Problems of Strategy in the Pacific and Indian Oceans by George G. Thomson, October 1970

Soviet Penetration into the Middle East by Wynfred Joshua, July 1970. Revised edition, October 1971 (Out of print)

Australian Security Policies and Problems by Justus M. van der Kroef, May 1970 (Out of print)

Detente: Dilemma or Disaster? by Gerald L. Steibel, July 1969 (Out of print)

The Prudent Case for Safeguard by William R. Kintner, June 1969 (Out of print)

Forthcoming

The Development of Strategic Weapons by Norman Polmar

AGENDA PAPERS

Edited by Frank N. Trager and William Henderson
With the assistance of Dorothy E. Nicolosi

Seven Tracks to Peace in the Middle East by Frank R. Barnett,
April 1975

Arms Treaties with Moscow: Unequal Terms Unevenly Applied?
by Donald G. Brennan, April 1975

Toward a US Energy Policy by Klaus Knorr, March 1975

*Can We Avert Economic Warfare in Raw Materials? US Agri-
culture as a Blue Chip* by William Schneider, July 1974